THE
COURAGEOUS
FOLLOWER

THE
COURAGEOUS
FOLLOWER

STANDING UP
TO AND FOR
OUR LEADERS

IRA CHALEFF

Berrett-Koehler Publishers
San Francisco

Berrett-Koehler Publishers, Inc.
155 Montgomery St.
San Francisco, CA 94104-4109
Tel: 415-288-0260   Fax: 415-362-2512

ORDERING INFORMATION
Individual sales. Berrett-Koehler publications are available through bookstores. They can also be ordered directly from Berrett-Koehler at the address above.

Quantity sales. Discounts for Berrett-Koehler publications are available on quantity purchases by corporations, associations, and others. For details, contact the "Special Sales Department" at the Berrett-Koehler address above.

Orders for college textbook/course adoption use. Please contact Berrett-Koehler Publishers at the address above.

Orders by U.S. trade bookstores and wholesalers. Please contact Publishers Group West, 4065 Hollis St., Box 8843, Emeryville, CA 94662; tel. 510-658-3453; 1-800-788-3123.

Printed in the United States of America

Printed on acid-free and recycled paper that meets the strictest state and U.S. guidelines for recycled paper (85 percent total recovered fiber including 15 percent post-consumer waste).

Library of Congress Cataloging-in-Publication Data
Chaleff, Ira.
    The courageous follower : standing up to and for our leaders / Ira Chaleff. -- 1st ed.
      p. cm.
    Includes bibliographical references and index.
    ISBN 1–881052–66–4 (alk. paper)
    1. Organizational sociology. 2. Organizational behavior. 3. Leadership.
4. Power (Social sciences) I. Title.
HM131.C65 1995
302.3'5--dc20   95-6952
                                    CIP

First Edition
    00 99 98 97 96 95   10 9 8 7 6 5 4 3 2 1

DEDICATION

THIS BOOK IS DEDICATED to all those who have found themselves formally in the role of a follower and who acted on the courage of their convictions despite strong external pressure and cultural inhibitions against doing so. Most of these acts go unnoticed and unsung. An exception was a contemporary set of courageous acts that occurred during and after the Gulf War.

The first act was by a United States Army field commander who refused to follow his superior's repeated orders to fire because he believed the position was occupied by other elements of his own army. He was right, and by refusing to comply saved his fellow soldiers' lives from "friendly fire." The second act was by the army officers reviewing the incident. They recognized the commander's refusal to obey orders as an act of courage, not insubordination, and rewarded it with a medal.

CONTENTS

4. THE COURAGE TO CHALLENGE   79

5. THE COURAGE TO PARTICIPATE
IN TRANSFORMATION   111

I THINK THAT THE AIM OF THE PERFECT COURTIER is so to win for himself the favor and mind of the prince whom he serves that he may be able to tell him, and always will tell him, the truth about everything he needs to know, without fear or risk of displeasing him; and that when he sees the mind of his prince inclined to a wrong action, he may dare to oppose him and in a gentle manner avail himself of the favor acquired by his good accomplishments, so as to dissuade him of every evil intent and bring him to the path of virtue.

The Book of the Courtier, 1516
Baldesar Castiglione
Contemporary of Niccolo Machiavelli

PREFACE

IF YOU SCROLL THROUGH THE SUBJECT CATALOGUE at the Library of Congress you will find the category "leadership" and hundreds of books on the subject. You will not find a category "followership" and you will only find a handful of articles and a book or two on the subject, tucked away under the leadership rubric. This is curious as there are many more followers in the world than leaders. Improving their performance would seem equally worthy of study as improving the performance of leaders.

I have been absorbed with the subject of followership most of my life, since becoming aware as a child of the systematic destruction of six million European Jews by the Nazis during World War II. In my heart, like so many others, I held the German people responsible, not just their leader Adolf Hitler. When I was seven or eight I made up games in which I rescued as many people as I could from the Germans' death camps. It was never enough.

How could a whole country follow a vicious leader to the logical conclusions of his psychosis? This mass support for a psychotic leader may well have created the contemptuous association my generation has with the term "follower."

Only later did I learn that one of the basic principles of Nazi ideology was the "Feuhrerprinzip"—the Leader Principle—"One people, one Reich, one leader," which portrayed Hitler as the ultimate source of power and justice. In the "Feuhrerstat"—the Leader State—the "Feuhrertreu"—those loyal to the leader under any circumstances—were the noblest of human beings. The leader was always right. Questioning the leader was raised to a crime of the highest order.

I also learned of the "White Rose," a painfully small group that tried arousing their fellow Germans against Nazi crimes. They quoted the philosopher Johann Gottlieb Fichte, "Thou shalt act as if on thee and thy deed depended the fate of all Germany and thou alone must answer for it." But this principle of accountable followership obviously failed horribly. It was not sufficiently woven into the fabric of the culture. How many other cultures would also fail if this trait were put to a severe test? How many are failing the test now?

In every age there are leaders and their followers who commit atrocities. At this writing, many of us are mystified by the mass killings in Bosnia and by our feelings of helplessness to affect the situation. Why do we feel helpless to influence these events we decry? At least partially it is because the further away we are from a situation in which power is being abused, the harder it is for us to influence it. Yet the closer we are to a situation in which power is being abused, the more we are at risk if we try to change it and the abuser turns on us. Thus, the people nearest to the event often let it grow unchecked. And the people farther away wring their hands.

Proximity and courage are the critical variables in the prevention of the abuse of power. With these variables in mind, I have written this book for and about the followers who serve closely to a leader. While it might speak most dramatically to the inner circle of a highly placed leader, the principles apply to the close followers of a leader in any size or type of organization, and at any level of the organization. I focus on the courage required to take advantage of proximity, as only with courage can we act quickly and early to ensure that the leader's power will be used well.

If we practice being courageous in our mundane interactions with leaders, we will be prepared if one day we are called upon to display extraordinary courage in our relationship with a leader. By weaving the principle of accountable followership into our culture at every level, the fabric will become strong enough to resist the periodic attempts of individual leaders to emboss it with their own martial coat of arms.

But it is not just at the extremes of human activity that these principles apply. The fabric is formed and reinforced in every organized activity of society from the youth group to the work place, from the church to the military, from the nonprofit to the corporation, from the local council to the national government.

As a teenager, I experienced the damage caused by the strong head of a youth organization who kept it alive through his dedication and energy, and simultaneously traumatized it through unchecked verbal and sexual abuse. In the socially idealistic sixties and human-potential movements of the seventies, I worked with groups dedicated to reforming the world and watched in dismay when their leadership's own use of power ceased to compare favorably to practices in the world they were seeking to change. As a management consultant to U.S. senators and representatives, I observe the difficulty many have in maintaining an atmosphere in which their staffs are willing to give them honest feedback about their leadership style. As a consultant to Fortune 500 companies and U.S. federal agencies, I see the inordinate weight given to a senior executive's slightest request, without regard to the effect it has on serving the customers who are supposed to drive the quality revolution.

The most capable followers in the world will fail if they gripe about their leaders but don't help them improve. As a follower, I am working to sustain the courage it requires to be honest in my relationships with leaders so I can tell them what they need to hear if they are to use their gifts effectively despite their inevitable human flaws. I now see that at those times when I have failed to provide a leader with needed perspective and balance, it was not for lack of perception but for lack of courage and skill. It was I who needed to change and grow as much as the leader. By not doing so I, along with the rest of the group, paid the price of dysfunctional leadership.

Like many followers, I am also a leader in my own right, and I am working to transform my own leadership attitudes that quash the creativity and participation of my staff. This doesn't come easy to me. Though I may wince, I find myself grateful when a courageous follower skillfully and tactfully confronts me and helps me visualize changes I might make to better serve the organization.

I first conceived the idea for this book ten years ago while reading M. Scott Peck's *People of the Lie*. I am indebted to him for raising the issue of irresponsible followership in his graphic analysis of the shameful massacre at My Lai by American soldiers in Vietnam. It framed my long search for understanding of the subject. This book is the fruit of my informal but deeply concerned and protracted observations, reading, and reflection on the leader-follower relationship.

Though the approaches and techniques I describe in the book for changing our relationships with leaders are often simple, they are offered with the understanding that changing ourselves or others is rarely easy. I have tried to emphasize the need for compassion and mutual respect in our relationships as followers and leaders.

Please be a courageous reader. This book is designed as a guide and a resource; don't follow it in a rote manner. While I encourage you to read the introduction and first chapter to get oriented to the subject, not all the remaining parts will be equally relevant to your current situation. Use the subchapter headings to locate the parts that are important to you.

This work is based on my personal experiences with both men and women in the leader role and the follower role. In my treatment of any specific issue, if I was not able to keep it gender-neutral, I somewhat arbitrarily chose one gender for the leader role and one for the follower role and stuck to that combination for that chapter. I must acknowledge, however, that gender issues sometimes complicate the already sensitive dynamics in the leader-follower relationship, and I have not attempted to deal with them in this work.

I am also aware of the inherent cultural biases which may render the model I present less relevant outside a contemporary middle-class, North American environment. I hope that some of the principles I explore will transcend the limits of my specific culture and speak to the broader human condition we all share.

Ultimately, the work that must be done to create new standards of relationship between followers and leaders begins within you and the experiences of your life. I invite you to explore this subject in your life as I am exploring it in mine.

Ira Chaleff
Washington, D.C.
February 1995

ACKNOWLEDGMENTS

I SHOWED THE FIRST THIN DRAFT OF THIS BOOK to my friend Steven Bosacker, an astute management thinker and, at the time, a chief of staff to a member of the U.S. Congress. His early encouragement of the work was crucial to my continuing the project. Other early readers who gave both encouragement and desperately needed criticism include Dr. Janet Poley, U.S. Representative Tim Penny, Dr. Jeff Fishel, Dr. Susan Hammond, Frank Gregorsky, Diane Thompson, Sara King, Kirk Stromberg, and my dear friend and fellow author, Olivia Mellan.

Readers of later drafts provided equally crucial encouragement and feedback: Duncan Campbell, Bill Schmidt, Dr. Jack J. Phillips, Jim Liebig, Major Don Zacherl, Laura Scott, Helen Foster, Frank Basler, Gordon MacKenzie, Prudence Goforth, General Walter Ulmer, and my friend who has seen me through good times and bad times as a leader and follower, Ron Hopkins. I am particularly thankful to Jim Liebig for challenging a key weakness in the manuscript so I could correct it, and to Bill Schmidt for urging me to emphasize "the common purpose" as the center of the leader-follower relationship.

In addition to inspiration and feedback, writers need space and time. I want to thank my old friend Robert Young for providing a cabin and swimming hole at an important juncture, as well as all the good people I met on repeated visits to the Pendle Hill Quaker study and contemplation center. I need to thank my partner, Kerry Gleeson, also a recent author, for his understanding of the time this project required and for the many things I have learned from him about leading and working with leaders. I want to acknowledge my wife, Carolyn, for assuming the role of "single parent" during the various times I went off on writing retreats, and thank her, my daughter, Lily, and my son, Sky, for being supportive of this project though it kept us from being together as much as we would have liked.

I also want to thank: Rick Shapiro and the other staff of the Congressional Management Foundation, who gave me hearty moral support throughout this project; my colleagues at the Institute for Business Technology, who have shared my excitement as the project developed; John Alexander at the Center for Creative Leadership for his support in various ways; Dr. David Mermelstein, who through tough, caring feedback has taught me a lot about myself and the process of transformation; my writing mentor, the novelist Carole Maso; Mary Lou Sumberg, whose caring and careful editing put a polish on my words; my extended family and friends, past and present, who have believed in me; and the many leaders, followers, colleagues, and clients from whom I have learned.

I am especially grateful to Steven Piersanti of Berrett-Koehler for recognizing the importance of this project in its rough, early stages and for giving me sound guidance on bringing out its full potential. It is my belief that he collaborates with angels to do his work. While contemporary authors don't usually thank God in their acknowledgments, Steven would be the first to agree this is an omission.

Lastly, I wish to thank those who gave me life, my grandparents and parents. This book is part of my effort to use that gift of life well.

INTRODUCTION

IN MANY ORGANIZATIONS TODAY, there is an important movement away from the extremes of all-powerful leaders and powerless, dependent followers. We hear much talk of "shared leadership," a helpful concept in softening the rigid demarcation lines often found between leaders and followers. But there is a limit to the usefulness of this concept. Despite the fact that many people experience visceral discomfort with the term "follower," it is not realistic to erase all distinctions between leaders and followers.

Instead, we need a dynamic model of followership that balances and supports dynamic leadership. We need a model that helps us embrace rather than reject the identity of follower because the model speaks to our courage, power, integrity, responsibility, and sense of service. This book proposes a proactive view of the follower's role, which brings it into parity with the leader's role. Parity is approached when we recognize that leaders rarely use their power wisely or effectively over long periods unless they are supported by followers who have the stature to help them do so.

In many situations, no matter how much partnership or empower-ment exists, the leader has ultimate authority and responsibility. The owner of a business, the commander of a fleet, the mayor or governor, a director of a nonprofit organization, the producer of a film, all have certain powers they retain for themselves and accountability that is not transferrable.

It is difficult to appreciate the external pressures on leaders until you have walked in their shoes, until you have had to make payroll, bring a squadron through safely, or respond to the outraged constituents who elected you. The internal pressures on leaders are often equally potent. "Ego-strength," one of the qualities that propels an individual to leadership, is reinforced in ways that can deform it into "ego-driven." If these pressures aren't managed well, with adroit help from followers, they can distort the leader's decision-making processes and interpersonal dynamics. Usually, the distortion will be in the direction of more authoritarian behavior and away from the partnering we desire.

How does a follower effectively support a leader and relieve these pressures? How does a follower become a "shaper" rather than simply an "implementer"? How does a follower contribute to leadership development rather than become a critic of leadership failings?

As in all human endeavor, many of us do some of these things quite naturally. But most of us can readily identify times we felt frustrated in our "second fiddle" situation as we watched our leaders make a mess of things, whether from the best of intentions or the worst. The increasingly egalitarian age we live in does not allow us to comfortably shirk responsibility and say, "Well, she's the boss!" We've grown beyond authoritarian models that strip followers of accountability. But we haven't necessarily grown fully comfortable with a new way of operating.

Most of us are leaders in some situations and followers in others. On one level we understand and fully accept this. You can't, by definition, have a world just of leaders! To think of leaders without followers is like thinking of teachers without students. Both are impossible. They are two sides of one process, two parts of a whole. Teachers and students form a learning circle around a body of knowledge or skills; leaders and followers form an action circle around a common purpose.

But on another level there seems to exist the deepest discomfort with the term "follower." It conjures up images of docility, conformity, weakness, and failure to excel. Often, none of this is the least bit true. The sooner we move beyond these images and get comfortable with the idea of *powerful* followers supporting *powerful* leaders, the sooner we can fully develop and test models for dynamic, self-responsible, synergistic relationships in our organizations.

If we are to attain the empowerment we crave, we must accept responsibility for both our own roles and the roles of our leaders. Only by accepting this dual responsibility do we ultimately accept responsibility for our organizations and the people they serve. There are three things we need to understand to fully assume this responsibility:

First, we must understand our own power and how to use it. As followers we have far more power than we usually acknowledge. We must understand the sources of our power, whom we serve, and what tools we have to carry forward the group's mission from our unique vantage point.

Second, we must appreciate the value of leaders and cherish the critical contributions they make to our endeavors. We must understand the forces that chisel away at their creativity, good humor, and resolve. We must learn how to minimize these forces and create a climate in which a leader's strengths are magnified, so a leader can better serve the common purpose.

Third, we must understand the seductiveness and pitfalls of the power of leadership. We are all familiar with Lord Acton's quote, "Power tends to corrupt and absolute power corrupts absolutely." We are all witnesses to the many examples that support its assertion. Yet we are like the person who has never taken hard drugs: though we can intellectually understand that they are addictive, we cannot appreciate their force. We must learn how to counteract this dark tendency of power.

The changes occurring in the world make it an opportune time to develop new models of followership. In the past, centralized organizations used relatively crude instruments and blunt force to coordinate resources in pursuit of their objectives. If you were building a pyramid, this method of organization worked terrifically. If you were laying a railroad, it also worked well. It even worked for awhile if you were building cars on an assembly line. Dominant leaders and compliant followers were able to get the job done. In information-age organizations, however, hundreds of decentralized units process and rapidly act on highly varied information within the design and purpose of the organization. This requires an entirely different relationship between leaders and followers.

Additionally, in both the West and the East, a new social contract is being formulated. In the largest organizations, we are no longer guaranteed employment. Our health benefits and retirement plans are being made portable. Leaders and organizations will no longer take care of us. Paternalism is gone. We need to take care of ourselves and each other.

In a deep way this is liberating. A central problem in the leader-follower relationship is its tendency to become a parent-child relationship, a relationship in which the follower is dependent and unable to relate to the leader on an equal footing.

A new model of followership can help us reorient ourselves and our relationships with leaders. I am choosing the image of the "courageous follower" to build a model of followership because courage is so antithetical to the prevailing image of followers and so crucial to balancing the relationship with leaders.

Courageous followership is built on the platform of courageous relationship. The courage to be right, the courage to be wrong, the courage to be different from each other. Each of us sees the world through our own eyes and experiences. Our interpretation of the world thus differs. In relationships we struggle to maintain the validity of our own interpretation while learning to respect the validity of other interpretations.

The danger in the leader-follower relationship is the assumption that the leader's interpretation must dominate. If this assumption exists on the part of either the leader or the follower, they are both at risk. The leader's openness to diversity, empowering others, breakthrough thinking, and being challenged and learning from followers will drop precipitously. Followers will abandon their unique perspectives and healthy dissension, which are at the heart of the creative process and innovation.

Contemporary leadership texts make compelling arguments for leaders to drive fear out of organizations, to share power, to invite feedback, to encourage participation. The leaders likely to read and respond to these arguments are the ones already open to change. What about those who cannot be their own agents of change, who do not walk the talk? I believe that courageous followers can and must be agents of change for such leaders.

But powerful socialization mechanisms, which served centralized bureaucracies well and taught followers to obediently follow, are still largely in force. The awesome shaping powers of school, organized religion, sports teams, the military, and large corporations are weakening, but still, whatever else they teach, they condition followers to obey. Expulsion for nonconformity is a very real threat. The conditioning begins at an age when children are still utterly dependent on their parents for survival and experience considerable anxiety about the consequences of not obeying. Our institutions play on this anxiety and, wittingly or not, reinforce it until followers often do become the timid creatures we emotionally reject identifying with.

We must examine this programming of the follower's role and envision what the role can become. What are our attitudes toward leaders? Where do our loyalties ultimately lie? What outcomes are worse than expulsion? What power do we have to support leaders who are striving to serve their group? And what obligation and power do we have to change things when higher loyalties are betrayed? How courageous do we dare to be?

We don't have a lot of cultural support for doing this. Our mythology focuses on hero-leaders who perform remarkable feats and successfully challenge villain-leaders. We lack common-man, common-woman heroes who stay true to their own lights while helping leaders follow theirs. Supportive "Number Twos" have not attracted much press coverage or six-figure publishing advances. Whistleblowers have fared considerably less well, their lives often seriously disrupted, with few rallying to their support. The time has come for leaders and followers to develop new models for relating to each other.

I will first explore the dynamics of the leader-follower relationship. What binds the leader and follower together? What are the underlying moral, emotional, and psychological forces at work? What are the respective powers each has in the relationship? I will then present a model of how courageous followers can improve that relationship for the benefit of themselves, their leaders, and the organization.

There are four dimensions in which a courageous follower operates within a group, and a fifth dimension outside of the group. The model will explore each of these dimensions as a way to compare our current followership practices with how we might develop the follower role.

THE FIVE DIMENSIONS OF COURAGEOUS FOLLOWERSHIP

THE COURAGE TO ASSUME RESPONSIBILITY

Courageous followers assume responsibility for themselves and the organization. They do not hold a paternalistic image of the leader or organization; they do not expect the leader or organization to provide for their security and growth, or to give them permission to act. Courageous followers discover or create opportunities to fulfill their potential and maximize their value to the organization. They initiate values-based action to improve the organization's external activities and its internal processes. The "authority" to initiate comes from the courageous follower's understanding and ownership of the common purpose, and from the needs of those the organization serves.

THE COURAGE TO SERVE

Courageous followers are not afraid of the hard work required to serve a leader. They assume new or additional responsibilities to unburden the leader and serve the organization. They stay alert for areas in which their strengths complement the leader's and assert themselves in these areas. Courageous followers stand up for their leader and the tough decisions a leader must make if the organization is to achieve its purpose. They are as passionate as the leader in pursuing the common purpose.

THE COURAGE TO CHALLENGE

Courageous followers give voice to the discomfort they feel when the behaviors or policies of the leader or group conflict with their sense of what is right. They are willing to stand up, to stand out, to risk rejection, to initiate conflict in order to examine the actions of the leader and group when appropriate. They are willing to deal with the emotions their challenge evokes in the leader and group. Courageous followers value organizational harmony and their relationship with the leader, but not at the expense of the common purpose and their integrity.

THE COURAGE TO PARTICIPATE
IN TRANSFORMATION

When behavior that jeopardizes the common purpose remains unchanged, courageous followers recognize the need for transformation. They champion the need for change and stay with the leader and group while they mutually struggle with the difficulty of real change. They examine their own need for transformation and become full participants in the change process as appropriate.

THE COURAGE TO LEAVE

Courageous followers know when it is time to separate from a leader and group. Self-growth or organizational growth may require a courageous follower to eventually leave even the most enlightened and effective of leaders. When leaders are ineffective or their actions are detrimental to the common purpose and they are not open to transformation, the need for separation becomes more compelling. Courageous followers are prepared to withdraw support from, even to disavow or oppose destructive leaders, despite high personal risk.

The world is fitfully evolving to a more egalitarian culture. Leadership and followership are evolving. As in any evolutionary process, the prospects for the emerging stage of development often look dubious. There will be times while reading this book when you might wince at suggested behaviors and think, "Get real!" For some leaders the suggested approach *will* be unreal. For others, who have allowed contemporary cultural changes to seep into their patterning, the approach presented here may be startling, but will also be fresh and welcome. The leader's reactions are of secondary importance, however, to the actions of the follower. That is why this book focuses on the courage of the follower; we are not talking about comfortable, risk-free behavior.

Most of us will have ample opportunity to experiment with and develop new models of courageous followership in the course of "ordinary" living. We will help our organizations compete more efficiently, make them more "employee-friendly," and help our community groups function more responsively.

But the extraordinary also occurs: the opportunity to help a leader make a bold peace initiative, the discovery of abusive practices that demand reversal, the chance to influence leadership practices that may bring an organization to a crossroads in choosing the values by which it will live. To the degree we have become strong and comfortable with new models of followership, those models will serve us well when we find ourselves in situations where the consequences are profound.

Whether we are dealing with the ordinary or extraordinary, the challenge a follower faces is significant. This book is designed to give the courageous follower the insights and tools needed to meet that challenge.

1

THE DYNAMICS OF THE LEADER-FOLLOWER RELATIONSHIP

I USED TO HAVE ASPIRATIONS to work closely with prominent leaders but found that when I was actually with them I would clutch, become tongue-tied, or engage more in flattery than dialogue. In doing this, I wasted whatever opportunity there may have been to develop a meaningful relationship with the leader in which we learned from each other.

When still in the "aspiring" state, I would look forward to being seated at the same table as the head of the organization at a company banquet. Later, as I discovered my nervousness about the interaction, I purposely avoided this close contact. Yet a colleague of mine, who was affable but not normally ingratiating, always aggressively sat himself next to the president of the company if he could, and was incredulous that others did not fight for the opportunity to bring themselves to the president's attention. For both my colleague and me, the mere fact of close contact with the leader produced changes in how we usually behaved with other people.

As a leader myself, I observed who would influence me and whom I was prone to ignore or dismiss. The people who influenced me from a lateral or subordinate position seemed to have a deep, natural sense of self-worth. They needed this as at times I could present a pretty gruff image, which would intimidate a less confident person. They were able to separate out this aspect of my personality and not interpret it as their own failing. They knew their specialties, observed and respected my strengths, supported my efforts, and spoke to me forthrightly when they thought I was off the mark. They also cared as much as I did about the organization's purpose and our success in achieving it.

In this chapter I examine the challenges we face in establishing and maintaining a true relationship with a leader. By "true" I mean a relationship in which we can comfortably meet a leader as one human being to another. In a true relationship, we are neither retiring nor fawning nor manipulative. We work together with mutual respect and honesty to achieve our common purpose.

THE COMMON PURPOSE AND CORE VALUES

Any organization is a triad consisting of leaders and followers joined in a common purpose. The purpose is the atomic glue that binds us. It gives meaning to our activities.

> **Followers and leaders both orbit around the purpose; followers do not orbit around the leader.**

Often the purpose exists and we come together around it. Sometimes the leader envisions it and draws us to it. At other times we formulate or redefine the purpose together. If the purpose is not clear and motivating, leaders and followers can only pursue their perceived self-interest, not their common interest. The process of clarifying purpose can mobilize a group, heal painful rifts, and help the group steer through treacherous passages. It is a critical act of strong leadership and courageous followership.

Equally fundamental are the group's shared values. Clarifying core values validates the purpose and determines how we will and how we won't pursue it. If the purpose is pursued in the context of decent human values, it serves as a guiding light in navigating our relationship with a leader. If the purpose intrinsically violates or is pursued in a way that violates decent human values, however, it is not an ethically valid guide. For example, revitalizing the Fatherland is a purpose we can use to guide our actions. Revitalizing the Fatherland by eliminating "undesirable types of people," however, nullifies its validity in determining appropriate action.

A common purpose pursued with decent values is the heart of the healthy leader-follower relationship.

THE PARADOX OF FOLLOWERSHIP

We are responsible. Whether we lead or follow, we are responsible for our own actions and we share responsibility for the actions of those whom we can influence.

All important social accomplishments require complex group effort and, therefore, leadership and followership. Both are necessary in the pursuit of a common purpose. Some believe that influence in the leader-follower relationship is largely one-way. This is far from true. Followers have great capacity to influence the relationship.

Just as a leader is accountable for the actions and performance of followers, so followers are accountable for their leaders. We must support leaders and, when necessary, help them correct their actions, just as they must support us and help us correct our actions. This is partnership. Both sides must be proactive. If we have followers who are partners with leaders, we will not have leaders who are tyrants.

Leadership may be informal and distributed throughout an organization. But formal leadership, which has final accountability and authority, is usually vested in an elected or appointed or self-proclaimed leader or small group. At the extremes, the formal leaders of a group may be wise or arrogant, servants or parasites, visionaries or demagogues. More commonly, leaders are a rich blend of strengths and weaknesses, of qualities that add and subtract value, and there is the potential for either side of their personalities to grow while in office. The quality and courage of followers influence which of the leader's characteristics will grow.

If we amplify our leaders' strengths and modulate their weaknesses, we are the gem cutters of leadership, coaxing out its full brilliance. If we amplify our leaders' weaknesses, we may stress existing fracture lines in their characters and these fracture lines may become fatal flaws. Followers who are closest to a leader carry pivotal responsibility; they markedly shape the tone and outcomes of a leader's tenure.

Courageous followership is full of paradox:

A courageous follower has a clear internal vision of service while being attracted to a leader who articulates and embodies its external manifestation.

Courageous followers remain fully accountable for their actions while relinquishing some autonomy and conceding certain authority to a leader.

A central dichotomy of courageous followership is the need to energetically perform two opposite roles: implementer and challenger of the leader's ideas.

There is inherent tension between the identity a follower derives from group membership and the individuation required to question and creatively challenge the group and its leadership.

Followers often benefit from the leader as mentor, learning crucial things, yet at the same time must be willing to teach the leader.

At times, courageous followers need to lead from behind, breathing life into their leader's vision, or even vision into the leader's life.

Senior followers often are important leaders in their own right and must integrate within themselves the perspectives of both leadership and followership.

The concept of a "courageous follower" appears to some to be an oxymoron but, if embraced, enables followers to join leaders fully as stewards of the group's trust.

WHO DOES A FOLLOWER SERVE?

"Follower" is not synonymous with "subordinate." A subordinate reports to an individual of higher rank and may in practice be a supporter, an antagonist, or indifferent. A follower shares a common purpose with the leader, believes in what the organization is trying to accomplish, and wants both the leader and the organization to succeed.

Like the leader, the follower is a steward of the resources an organization can draw on to carry out its work. The resources of a group include its leaders. Thus, a follower is a leader's steward every bit as much as a leader is the follower's steward.

We can perform our role as followers at different levels:

> At the purest level, we serve those whom the organization exists to serve—its members, clients, constituents, customers, communities—often called stakeholders because of their stake in the outcome of the group's actions.

> Below that, and quite functionally, we simultaneously serve the organization's stakeholders and its leaders, with no conflict of interest.

> Below that, we serve the leaders and ourselves but not the stakeholders. While we may be rewarded for this in the short run, we sow the seeds of the organization's failure.

> At the lowest level, we serve the leaders while permitting them to harm the organization and its stakeholders through corruption, and we participate in that corruption ourselves.

If we serve only ourselves and not the leaders or the stakeholders, we are not followers but opportunists siphoning off the energy of the group to serve our own agendas.

LOYALTY OF A FOLLOWER

In the past, when relationships were more stable and lifelong social contracts were the norm, loyalty was unquestioningly given—to the clan, to the feudal lord, to the sole employer. Unquestioning loyalty is, of course, fraught with moral peril. Today, relationships are constantly shifting and loyalty is problematic—who deserves it and why? Yet the lifting of cultural pressure to give blind loyalty allows us to the freedom to make conscious moral choices based on our core values.

Placing our loyalty somewhere is an important act of identity. We can place it in ourselves and often this is important to help us stay a difficult course. But if we place no loyalty outside ourselves we become a kind of brigand, justifying any action regardless of its cost to others.

Leaders and followers who find themselves in constantly shifting configurations need to find a mutual place for their loyalty that transcends the impermanence of their relationship, yet bonds them in a framework of trust. This is the importance of the contemporary emphasis on vision, values, and mission statements: well formulated, these define the loyalty that leaders and followers pledge to those who have a stake in the group.

The values statement evokes a circumscribed loyalty—to fairness, to quality, to honesty, to service, to a common purpose. Circumscribed loyalty to worthy values avoids the pitfalls of unlimited loyalty and may be an evolutionary step forward. Both leaders and followers are entering into a contract to pursue the common purpose within the context of their values. The loyalty of each is to the purpose and to helping each other stay true to that purpose.

If leadership and followership are both forms of stewardship, then loyalty is correctly directed to the organization's purpose and its stakeholders. It appropriately includes and embraces the principles, people, and environments affected by the organization's actions. Once appropriate loyalty is clarified, it can inform our decisions to support or challenge a leader's agenda.

POWER IN THE LEADER-FOLLOWER RELATIONSHIP

Wherever an organization lies on the spectrum from "hierarchical" to "shared" leadership, there is always some power vested in the leaders and some in the followers. In shared leadership, the power is more balanced although one faction may accumulate power over other factions. In an autocratic hierarchy, power appears to reside almost entirely with the leader until something occurs that causes the followers to depose the leader and reclaim their power.

The situation in which power appears to reside entirely with the leader is very dangerous both for the follower, who can be ruined at the leader's whim, and for the leader, whose followers become sycophantic.

Sycophants act according to what they have learned is expected of them in a situation. They do not observe or think well for themselves, and often fail to take appropriate actions. This hurts the leader and the organization.

As followers, our formal powers are unequal to the leader's, and we must learn to participate effectively in the relationship despite this. We may have far more power than we imagine, however, and too often fail to exercise the power we do have. It is critical for followers to connect with their power and learn how to use it. To maintain and strengthen power, it must be used; otherwise, it will wither.

The sources of a follower's power are varied:

the power of purpose, the strength that comes from commitment to the common good;

the power of knowledge, the possession of skills and resources the organization and its leadership value and do not want to lose;

the power of personal history, a record of successes and unassailable contributions to the leader and the organization;

the power of faith in self, belief in our observations and intentions, in our integrity and commitment;

the power to speak the truth, as we see it, to the leadership;

the power to set a standard that influences others, to model values and behavior for the leader and group members;

the power to choose how to react in a situation regardless of what is done or threatened by others;

the power to follow or not follow in a given direction;

the power of relationships, of networks of people who know and trust us;

the power to communicate through a variety of channels;

the power to organize others of like mind;

the power to withdraw support if the leadership's actions violate our values.

If we are to be effective partners with leaders, it is important to remember that as followers we possess our own power, quite apart from the reflected power of the leader.

VALUE OF THE FOLLOWER

Follower is not a term of weakness, but the condition that permits leadership to exist and gives it strength. Dynamic followers recognize their own aspirations in the leader's vision. They follow their own light, which the leader intensifies. They give 110 percent, not because the leader "motivates them" but because they are inspired—the spirit of the activity is within them. They are interdependent with, not dependent on, the leader. They add value to both themselves and the leader through this relationship.

The value of a follower is measured by how completely the follower helps the leader and organization pursue their common purpose within the context of their values. Certain characteristics help to do this:

Effective followers are cooperative and collaborative, qualities essential to all human progress.

Trusted followers integrate their ego needs sufficiently into their communal responsibilities to serve rather than compete with the leader.

Well-balanced followers are less prone to the pitfalls that await leaders with strong egos and can serve as guides around these pitfalls.

Caring followers perceive the needs of both the leader and other group members and try to form a bridge between them.

We retain our value as followers to the degree we remain true to those whom our organization serves, to the degree we are courageous in doing this. If we bend to the will of a leader when it conflicts with the interests of our stakeholders, or if we bend to the will of our stakeholders when it conflicts with the higher values of humanity, our value is greatly diminished.

COURAGE OF THE FOLLOWER

Courage is the great balancer of power in relationships. An individual who is not afraid to speak and act on the truth as she perceives it, despite external inequities in a relationship, is a force to be reckoned with.

Courage implies risk. If there is no risk, courage is not needed. Life, of course, is full of risk at every turn, at every moment. We usually structure our lives to reduce risk to an acceptable level. Courage requires a willingness to consciously raise our level of risk, at least in the short term.

A priest must be willing to tell the bishop that moral turpitude is being covered up in his see. An aide must be willing to tell the governor that her policies will cause severe hardship. A mid-level manager must be willing to tell senior management that by only paying lip service to Total Quality they are undermining its implementation.

While silence may appear the safe choice, it often leaves our relationships with leaders or peers sapped of the vitality that honest dialogue produces. A follower needs the courage of an inquisitive child who asks questions without fear, but also needs the courage of an adult who bears the responsibility for a family. The family's need for security may clash with the need to risk that security for higher principles. This is a core issue, for without the willingness to risk on this profound level, we won't speak the truth. From where can we draw the courage to speak and act our truth and not be inhibited from doing so by the potential consequences?

On a practical level, if our livelihood depends on our position with the leader, it is healthy for us to develop contingency plans should we fall out of favor. Another job opportunity, money in the bank to support us for a year, a working spouse or partner, any of these can provide a safety net that makes our leap of courage less intimidating. If our career will be jeopardized by a clash with the leader, plotting alternate career paths can reduce the potential severity of the consequences. Being prepared to be fired is the antidote to silencing ourselves.

On a deeper level, each of us may find our own courage springs from a different source:

> our religious beliefs;
>
> our philosophy;
>
> a role model;
>
> a vision of the future;
>
> a vow made from past experience;
>
> an event that tested us;
>
> a conviction we hold;
>
> our values;
>
> our empathy for others;
>
> our self-esteem;
>
> commitment to our comrades;
>
> outrage felt toward injustice.

If we are clear on the source of our courage, it prepares us to accept the consequences of our actions. To act courageously, we may not need to free ourselves from fear, but to experience our fear in the context of our source of courage. If you have ever been in a situation you believed was truly dangerous, you know the intensity of the emotional energy generated by fear. Suppressing the energy contained in this fear and "rising above it" is one strategy. Another strategy, perhaps more effective, is to let the fear rise up fully, acknowledge it, and then channel the energy locked within that fear into the service of our principles and goals. If our principles and goals are clear, enormous self-empowerment can occur.

We probably have to fail a few times before we succeed. The first time we are confronted with the use of raw power, with its assumptions and attitude and force, it is so startling that we may well flinch or freeze. We may need to go away and prepare ourselves to meet it again.

Our "courage muscle" will develop to the degree we exercise it. If we exercise it when the risks are small, it will be strong enough to meet the challenge when the risks are large. Ultimately, there are no formulas for courage: we develop it through determination and practice, self-forgiveness when we fail, and growth when we learn.

BALANCE THROUGH RELATIONSHIP

In different situations, different qualities are most needed and productive—courage, diplomacy, consistency, firmness—all are virtues which have their place. But any virtue taken to an extreme and used in the wrong situation can become a vice: courage becomes recklessness, diplomacy becomes appeasement, consistency becomes rigidity, firmness becomes brutality.

As a leader acquires power, qualities that contribute to success are affirmed and reinforced and may begin to be relied on excessively. When a leader receives only positive feedback, these qualities can be reinforced to the point where they become dysfunctional. Similarly, flaws that may be of minor consequence when power is small can become magnified with the increase of power. In either case, the leader's talents may be eclipsed by weaknesses.

Dynamic leaders are the spark, the flame that ignites action. With vision, they generate and focus power. But followers are the guarantors of the beneficial use of that power. Dynamic leaders may use power well, but they cannot be the guarantors. In their passion, their expansiveness, their drive, dynamic leaders are prone to excess: a deal too large, a bottom line too important, a cause too righteous, an image too pure, a lifestyle too rich, an enemy too hated, a bridge too far. We provide the balance *if* we can stand up to our leaders.

At the heart of balance is the dual nature of the universe—I and the other—and the necessity for relationship. Genuine relationships will not tolerate extremes, which become abusive. The key to personal balance for leaders is the quality of their relationships with followers. Honest, open relationships will provide a steady stream of uncensored feedback. It is only through this feedback that leaders can accurately perceive and modulate their behavior.

Because of the unknowns, it takes courage for us to be open and direct with a leader while building a relationship.

How open is this leader willing to be with anyone?

How open can I be about myself?

Do I know how to read this person yet?

How does this individual respond to feedback?

If an issue is emotionally laden for me, how do I know my concern isn't exaggerated, or that I'll present it well?

How intense will the leader's reaction be?

What are the potential consequences for my career?

If we are not willing to risk whatever relationship we have built with a leader by providing honest feedback, we instead risk losing the whole dream for which we have both been working. We will grow more cynical about the leader, and the leader will grow increasingly unreal about the impact of his behavior. Two essential elements of relationship are developing trust and then using that trust to speak honestly when appropriate; one without the other is meaningless. The challenge for the courageous follower is to maintain a genuine relationship with the leader, not the pseudorelationship of the sycophant.

MATURE RELATIONSHIPS

Oddly enough, one of the challenges followers often face is helping leaders develop tolerance, decency and, in a sense, maturity. All humans struggle with the need to grow up, to accept that the rest of the world is not here to serve us, that people are going to differ with us, and that this is okay. The world soon teaches most of us these lessons, and we find ways of coping with our younger egocentric view of life even if we do not fully transform it.

When skill and circumstances combine to put us in a position of formal leadership, our early egocentric impulses are vulnerable to reemergence. If, as too often happens, leaders are surrounded by followers who kowtow to them, the immature parts of their personality, which have not been fully transformed, tend to regain dominance.

If the immature aspects of a leader's personality appear with increased frequency, this leaves us in the odd and difficult position of serving a leader who is competent, even brilliant in some dimensions, and a spoiled brat in other respects. The internal confusion and conflict that a follower may feel when confronted by the discrepancy between the mature and immature traits of a leader should not be underestimated: Is this brilliant, sometimes abusive leader deserving of my support or not?

This would not be such a difficult question if we felt empowered to challenge a leader about the immature behavior while supporting the mature skills and judgment he brings to the group. If our behavior is disruptive to the group, the leader is expected to raise the issue with us; similarly, we need to break the taboo against our raising behavior issues with the leader.

It is difficult to break the taboo because our early conditioning about leaders takes place in childhood, at home and school, where others are held responsible for our behavior but we are not held responsible for theirs. The power of our early conditioning is so strong that for most of us it is an act of courage to confront a leader about counterproductive behavior, instead of an ordinary act of relationship.

As in so many aspects of relationship, if we have difficulty with a leader who displays immaturity it is because we also have issues with maturity.

Too often, because of our sense of powerlessness, we complain protracted-ly to others about a leader's behavior instead of taking effective action. We do not serve the leader or organization well by immaturely whining about a leader's behavior instead of confronting the leader and participating in a process of mutual development.

It requires a courageous follower to confront a powerful leader about immature behavior. The situation can resemble confronting a young child holding a loaded gun; you may be shot persuading the child to put it down. It requires a skillful follower to confront a leader in a way that simultaneously respects the accomplished adult, preserves the adult's self-esteem, and challenges the immature behavior.

DIFFERENCES IN ELEVATION

Overcoming the sometimes very large differences in position within an organization can be a challenge in establishing a true relationship with a leader. Though we may work closely with the leader, the difference in the relative status or elevation of our positions can form a chasm in the rela-tionship. The sources of an elevation gap are varied:

The leader has been elected and the follower has been hired.

The leader founded the organization.

The leader owns the company.

The leader is considerably older and has held many elevated positions.

The leader holds a formal senior rank.

The leader is wealthy.

The leader has made major contributions to the organization.

The leader is widely regarded as a genius, a hero, or a celebrity.

These conditions may prompt us to think, "Who am I to question this person?" and disregard our perceptions or interpretations of events. We must stay highly alert to this reflex reaction and question it carefully. If it is the premise of our relationship we will fail both ourselves and the leader.

Warren Bennis, the great student and teacher of leadership, reports that 70 percent of followers will not question a leader's point of view even when they feel the leader is about to make a mistake. From their elevated positions leaders are prone to losing touch with the common reality. This is sometimes referred to as "the king's disease." Leaders are often dependent on the perceptions of followers to reconnect them to external realities.

If we have thoughtfully considered the merits of our observations, our challenge is to rise above the intimidating nature of the difference in elevation and present our ideas. Speaking forthrightly to an "elevated" leader is not presumptuous; it is an essential part of courageous followership.

FINDING EQUAL FOOTING
WITH THE LEADER

To look a leader in the eye and credibly deliver unpalatable observations or sharply differing opinions requires an internal sense of equal worth. Metaphorically, a pygmy cannot look a giant in the eye. Followers usually cannot match up to a leader's external qualities, such as the trappings of formal power, and must find their equal footing on intellectual, moral, or spiritual ground. How can we do this?

If we remember and speak to our common humanity, we need not be seduced, dazzled, or intimidated by the symbols of higher office. Neither we nor the leaders we support are our titles, whether this be secretary, boss, president, or emperor. We are human beings who pass through this existence with gifts and needs, anxieties and dreams, strengths and vulnerabilities. If we, as leaders and followers, remember our common nature, we will deal with each other out of mutual respect, not out of disdain or awe.

We need to closely observe ourselves in the presence of power to see how we behave. If we find ourselves speaking or acting with exaggerated deference, we are relating to the title, not to the person carrying it. If we observe ourselves being even subtly obsequious toward a leader, we should try to look past the title, trappings, and power of office to see the human being occupying the office. Who is the leader outside of this specific role?

Where has he come from?

What are his values?

Does his private persona differ from his professional one?

Does he feel supported or lonely?

Is he genuinely confident or perhaps masking insecurity?

Can he be playful?

Does he have a sense of serving a higher ideal or power?

Can we envision him as a parent, a son, a husband?

What failures and tragedies has he experienced?

What are his fears?

What are his aspirations?

Depending on how private the leader is, we may not be able to answer all these questions. And the answers are not as important as our ability to touch the leader's humanity. We need to demythologize leaders, to see them holistically, to be able to identify with their pain and joy so we can talk to them as one human being to another. We need to be able to comfortably ask ourselves the question, "How can I help this fellow human being whose lot has been cast together with mine?" As we answer this, we affirm the worth we bring to the relationship and find our equal footing.

WHEN THE LEADER ISN'T AN EQUAL

A different challenge exists when a leader isn't as qualified for the role as a follower or, in a sense, isn't the follower's equal. There are many circumstances in which this can occur:

organizational politics,

discrimination,

diversity values and policies,

rotational assignments,

seniority promotion,

family ownership,

election,

appointment,

high public profile,

connections,

amiability and charm.

When the most capable person is not the leader, a courageous follower faces several challenges. Most important is to deal with our own feelings about the matter. We often find it difficult to work for someone who is slower than we are, who fails to fully and rapidly grasp situations confronting the organization. Rather than feeling intimidated by their position, we may have difficulty masking our disdain. There may be bitterness if we hoped for the number one position ourselves.

We may also find ourselves in situations in which we must decide whether to cover for the leader or to publicly let the leader appear unprepared and unknowledgeable. We may experience ego-based conflict or ethical confusion about this.

Our workload often increases if the leader falls short of the role. Not only do we assume parts of what should be the leader's role, we also spend extra time educating the leader through memos and briefings. We usually do this for a lot less money and recognition than the leader is receiving. Our resentment can run high.

As difficult as it may be in this situation, our guiding principle should remain service to the organization. It is important to acknowledge our feelings and frustrations, but if we are committed to the common purpose, we will keep working with our leader for its accomplishment. We will use our talent and competencies to help the leader grow and succeed. As long as the leader is giving his best energy to the role, he deserves our private and public support. And it's surprising how much we can learn from even the leaders who don't excel.

Sometimes it is simply that a capable person is given a job for which he has little experience. A newly elected legislator may have a great vision but be an ingenue on how to craft passable legislation. A seasoned aide may need to guide the legislator through the nuances of the issues and politics and the labyrinths of the policy-making process. Eventually, the legislator will master the subject and the process.

The mark of a great leader is the development and growth of followers. The mark of a great follower is the growth of leaders.

TRUST

Leadership surveys show that trust is the single most important factor on which followers evaluate a leader. The reverse is equally true although the word "reliability" is often substituted when speaking of followers. Reliability is a composite of trust and competence, and a leader needs to experience both in a follower. Competence itself, while valued, can be threatening if the leader senses that the follower is motivated more by a personal agenda than by a desire to support the leader and group.

Trust is essential in the leader-follower relationship if followers are to serve and influence the leader and organization. Yet sometimes it is elusive. How is trust won?

> **Trust is a subtle state between two people formed from an assessment of each other's internal motives and external actions—if either are questionable trust does not gel.**

> **The gelling agents of trust are our word and the judgment we display in our actions.**

> **To earn trust we must go to great lengths to keep our word and, if we cannot keep it, we must communicate this as soon as possible.**

> **To maintain trust we must listen carefully to both external signals and our inner voice, which quietly warn us against actions that may be in poor judgment.**

Trust is a quality of relationship that can quickly return to its fluid, uncertain state in response to events and perceptions. Often we sense the change in trust before anything specific has been said or done about it, much as we sense an oncoming storm. If we sense a weakening of trust, we should make aggressive efforts to find out why, as it is the foundation of our relationship. It may be that we appear to have violated trust when we have not. In this case we should take great pains to clarify the situation, using any available documentation to dispel doubt.

If we have, indeed, violated trust through poor judgment or otherwise, the instinct to rationalize it can deliver a death knell to the relationship. Only by genuinely accepting responsibility for our actions and doing what we can to alleviate their consequences can we begin repairing trust.

If we have given genuine cause for trust to be lowered, it may dismay us to find how much time and contribution to the group is required before the breech is healed. A strong commitment to achieving the common purpose will be needed to sustain us through a difficult period.

FOLLOWERS AS LEADERS

In different situations, at different times, we are all followers or leaders. The best way to learn to lead is to work closely with a capable leader. But whether or not the leader is a positive role model, to the degree we are courageous followers we prepare ourselves to be courageous leaders.

Even as we follow, we often are simultaneously expected to lead others in a chain of authority. The dual role of follower and leader gives us ample opportunity to learn to perform better in both roles. It is an art to move fluidly between these roles and remain consistent in our treatment of others.

By staying aware of our reactions to those we follow, we learn to be more sensitive to our effect on those we lead.

By staying aware of our reactions to those we lead, we learn to be more sensitive in our efforts to support those we follow.

By modeling good leadership with our own followers, we can often influence our leaders. They observe us in our roles and borrow from our successes as we do from theirs. If we cannot influence our leader, we can transform even a miserable relationship into a rich learning opportunity if we use it to learn what demotivates followers and commit to not repeating these mistakes ourselves.

To effectively support a leader we often need to create our own support, our own group to execute that part of the mission with which we are entrusted. There is a danger we will be perceived as empire building if the team we create is especially strong. While leaders value our creating top-notch operations, they may also feel threatened by it. Our intention is of the essence. If we are genuinely serving the organization and its stakeholders, we won't use our strength to thwart the leader's initiatives or jockey for the leader's position. Our team will know they serve the common purpose, not us.

In the dance of leaders and followers we change partners and roles throughout our lives. With each new partner we must subtly adjust our movements and avoid the others' toes. If we are leading we must lead and if we are not we must follow, but always as a strong partner. We constantly learn from each other and improve our gracefulness in a wide diversity of styles and tempos.

WORKING WITH OTHER FOLLOWERS

While examining the leader-follower relationship it is important to bear in mind that the dynamics are much more complex than those between two individuals. There are usually at least several followers who are close to the leader, and the interaction between followers profoundly affects the group. Trust between the members of this group is as critical as trust between a leader and follower.

As in a family, there are issues of alliances and shifting alliances, favoritism and perceived favoritism, treatment according to birth order and gender, competing needs and demands for attention, differing styles and invidious comparisons, and limited resources. If these issues can be managed, the group will find strength in both diversity and unity.

There are at least two broad dimensions in these group relationships that courageous followers must stay alert to—how followers relate to each other and how they relate collectively to the leader.

How followers relate to each other:

Staying alert to the individual needs of each member brings us into collaborative unity rather than fractious competitiveness.

Appreciating our differences enables us to utilize those differences in the service of the common purpose.

Respecting each other's boundaries allows us to cross them by mutual consent without triggering turf warfare.

Building strong lateral communication and coordination among ourselves enables us to accomplish our functions.

Participating in creative thinking about issues instead of rigidly defending our positions invites the power of synergy into the group.

Remembering whom we serve will help us find common ground when we seem to be splitting into factions.

If we need to compete, it is best to outdo each other in forwarding the common purpose rather than in undermining each others' efforts.

Being willing to both lead and follow our peers, as the situation warrants, permits competency-based leadership.

How followers relate to the leader:

A follower's need to shine for the leader at the expense of the other stars in the group will cause stellar explosions in the group dynamics.

When presenting our counsel to the leader, we will earn both our peers' and the leader's trust if we also present full and fair descriptions of our peers' positions.

When followers bring their internal squabbles to the leader, it drains the leader and evokes impatient and poorly thought-out responses.

If a leader plays one follower against another, we need to resist the attractiveness of temporarily being in favor, and work collectively to change the dynamic.

When our peers act courageously toward the leader, it is critical that we support them and do not leave them out on the proverbial limb alone.

An effective follower stays sensitive to the complex dynamics within the leader's close support group. The dance has now become a lively reel, and we pay attention to all the whirling partners continuously changing positions within the dance's framework.

2

THE COURAGE
TO ASSUME
RESPONSIBILITY

 THE MOST FREQUENT COMPLAINT I HEAR from leaders is that they would like their staff members to assume more responsibility for the organization and initiate ideas and action on their own. While there are often very good reasons the staff members don't do this, embedded either in the leader's style or the organizational culture, it is interesting to hear that most leaders want their staff to take more initiative. They don't want to be the only one leading.

When I was at the University of California at Berkeley in the early sixties, a confrontation between the police and students erupted over the subject of free speech. The confrontation happened in the student plaza while the ad hoc student leadership and the administration negotiated the issues elsewhere. I was one of the hundreds of followers supporting the student leadership. By nightfall hundreds of police and thousands of students on both sides of the issue had amassed. The atmosphere was growing ugly with stink bombs and epithets being hurled at the demonstrators. It looked like the helmeted police would charge into the demonstrators to break up the sit-in. There was a person who was blind and children in the crowd. I was concerned that people would be hurt.

Joan Baez, the folk singer and political activist, was performing at the Greek theater on another part of campus that evening. She had recently achieved national fame. I called the hotel where celebrities stay in Berkeley and left her a message describing the situation. I asked her to come to the site of the confrontation, expressing the hope that by having a prominent figure present more restraint would be exercised and violence could be prevented. Though she didn't know me, she responded and appeared a little while later. While she made her presence known, each side restrained itself until a settlement was reached and everyone voluntarily dispersed. I learned the power of taking initiative without formal authority.

Unfortunately, I have not always assumed that much responsibility. Recently, I found myself disappointed by the quality of meetings my company held. The meetings consumed a lot of expense and time as people came from two continents, yet seemed to cover the same ground each year in an uninspiring format. I complained about it to the organization's founder and president, but did nothing else to change it.

Then I had the opportunity to use a self-assessment instrument and was startled to find how disaffected I had become with the president. This flew in the face of my self-image as a positive, contributing team member. I was challenged to assume responsibility for the situation rather than complain while it deteriorated.

I drafted a memo to the other participants in the company meetings and told the president that I intended faxing it to each of them. He supported the initiative. The memo explained what a terrific opportunity I saw in our annual meetings and offered a creative idea for taking better advantage of the meetings. I asked for their feedback. Nearly all replied, several with ideas of their own which I felt improved on mine. Out of this process, and to the president's delight, we constructed a new, stimulating, and valuable format for part of the meeting.

By assuming responsibility for our organization and its activities, we can develop a true partnership with our leader and sense of community with our group. This is how we maximize our own contribution to the common purpose. Assuming responsibility requires courage because we then become responsible for the outcomes—we can't lay the blame for our action or inaction elsewhere.

But before we can assume responsibility for the organization, we must assume responsibility for ourselves. I had to recognize my disaffection and do something to change it. I had to assume responsibility for my own growth. We cannot remain static ourselves and expect to improve the organization.

In this chapter I explore the responsibility a courageous follower takes for self-development and for the development of the organization. Though we coordinate our activities as appropriate, we also take actions independently of the leader to forward our common purpose.

SELF-ASSESSMENT

Assuming responsibility for our personal development begins with self-examination. We cannot know in which direction we need to grow until we first know where we are. Courageous followers do not wait for performance reviews (strained events that these usually are anyway); they assess their own performance.

In addition to evaluating their job "competencies," courageous followers also examine the more illusive subject of their relationships with teammates and leaders. If charity begins at home, development in the relationship between followers and leaders begins in a follower's vestibule: a follower's issues with authority are the other side of a leader's issues with power.

Our relationship to authority is so deeply ingrained that it is difficult to be fully aware of our beliefs and postures vis-à-vis leaders. For our entire childhoods, at home and school, those in authority had tremendous power to dictate to us. We learned to survive by complying with, avoiding, or resisting those authorities. The strategies we adopted became patterns for future behavior and influence our attitudes toward our current leaders.

Most work environments in adulthood reinforce our childhood relationship to authority. We must strive for greater awareness of our own beliefs, attitudes, and patterns of behavior toward authority, and look at their consequences. For example:

> **Challenging a specific leader on a specific subject may be healthy, but a pattern of challenging all leaders on all subjects is not. A rebellious, alienated follower will never earn the trust to meaningfully influence a leader.**

> **A follower's deferential language and demeanor toward a leader may be appropriate, but strained subservience or chronic resentment are not. A follower who is too subservient and eager to please authority cannot provide the balance a leader requires to use power well.**

> **Clamming up when a leader interrupts us in a raised voice may have been necessary at home or school, but serves us and the leader poorly now. Tolerating disrespect for our voice and views will reinforce the behavior and weaken the relationship.**

It is important to move beyond viewing a leader as a good parent or bad parent, a good king or bad king, a hero or villain in our world. If we become aware of such attitudes, our challenge is to learn to relate to the leader on a different basis. By paying attention to how we interpret the leader's actions, to the feelings that interpretation evokes in us, and to the behaviors we employ to cope with those feelings, we can loosen our grasp on the mechanisms we once needed for survival. We can begin to examine what other choices we have as adults for relating effectively to authority.

ELICITING FEEDBACK

While self-assessment is important, finding out how others see us is equally vital. Courageous followers overcome their reticence to hear "criticism"; they learn to encourage honest feedback. Though we have experiences or images of "bosses" giving us streams of criticism about specific tasks, in fact many do not provide feedback on the more fundamental issues they may have with us. They find it too uncomfortable to do so. They, too, can lack courage in relationships, despite their positional superiority.

Courageous followers draw the leader out despite discomfort on either of their parts:

> "Nobody does everything perfectly. What should I work on so I can do the job better?"

If we receive negative feedback, however tenuous, we should encourage it with statements like:

> "That's useful for me to know—can you tell me more about that?"

This emboldens the leader, who may be testing the water to see if we really do want to hear this. Once a spirit of open communication is established, a courageous follower probes further:

> "Are you concerned about any other aspects of my performance, which may be even more fundamental?"

If we can remain interested and avoid becoming defensive, we can learn crucial things about ourselves and the leader. We should ask for clarification and examples until we are very clear about what change would be desirable.

If the feedback we receive is about an issue on which the leader or others have previously confronted us, hearing further feedback on the subject may raise our understanding of the need to address it, and strengthen our resolve to do so. By eliciting feedback we make sure that we, not others, hear about our perceived flaws and that we are in a strong position to consider what to do about them.

PERSONAL GROWTH

Self-assessment and feedback help us determine in what ways it would be desirable for us to change, to grow. Growth requires courage; it is a continuous process of exposing our vulnerable areas, areas where we have not developed mastery. Growth also requires exploring what the Jungians call our "dark" side. This is uncomfortable to do. Yet the courage to assume responsibility includes responsibility for the parts of us that we'd rather not have the world look at too closely. If we are to contain or transform our leader's dark side, we had better become familiar with our own. We must learn to support our urge toward growth in its contest with the equally powerful urge to protect our self-image.

Personal growth often involves emotional struggle. We should be prepared for that struggle and not try to shut it down at the first signs of discomfort. The knowledge that we may feel worse before we feel better is important and enables us to stick with the lessons we need to learn. Supportive relationships or groups help us get through periods of emotional trial. Structured development programs, counseling, and mentor relationships all provide vehicles and support systems for internal growth.

We also need external growth opportunities. There is often ample room for growth within our current position if we assertively seek it. Working closely with a competent leader is itself a primary growth opportunity. At some point, however, it may be desirable to move away from the comfort of our current role to test ourselves in a new, unproven role. In an age when organizations no longer make lifelong commitments to employees, we must chart our own career growth.

If we shy away from discomfort, we will never grow.

If we seek challenge, we will continuously grow, often in unexpected ways.

Once again, we are responsible. We must be self-advocates for both our internal and external growth.

SELF-MANAGEMENT

We are also responsible for self-management. Our success at self-management creates both the credibility and resources to initiate changes that will improve the organization.

A key to self-management is personal organization. A follower who is not well organized will too often be unprepared, miss deadlines, submit faulty work, or otherwise fail to meet the leader's expectations. If a leader is frustrated with a follower's performance, it is difficult to remain open to the follower's advice and consultation.

Senior followers often lead others. If senior followers lack strong organizational skills, this affects the performance of their teams. If a team struggles to meet even their minimum responsibilities, they will certainly not have the energy to engage in new, creative initiatives.

Self-management encompasses the nuts and bolts of effective leadership or followership. It is mundane. It is pedestrian. Yet self-management is a critical skill, and a courageous follower must be prepared to do the hard work involved in being personally well organized.

There are several areas in which we must strive for a high degree of self-organization:

> The way information, requests, and responses flow in and out of our work environment must be clearly established and maintained.

> The tools, materials, and information needed to perform a function must be easily accessible and well maintained.

> Procedures must be in place to ensure the appropriate safeguarding of information and materiel.

> The criteria and measurements by which work will be judged need to be clearly understood and monitored.

> Complex activities should be analyzed and arranged to minimize redundancies and maximize utilization of resources.

Work needs to be scheduled to manage the competing demands on our own and others' time, and the schedule respected.

Requests for service or action should be recorded and trackable to allow for follow-through and timely closure.

Work should be appropriately delegated and delagatees developed and trusted so we do not become a bottleneck in the organization's processes.

If we are not naturally strong in these areas we must assume responsibility for improving our skills. The most common stumbling block is the feeling we do not have time to get ourselves better organized. Yet often, it is the lack of organization that is eating up our time. We must give self-organization attention now, not at some elusive point in the future. We must take time out to sharpen the ax or we'll exhaust ourselves trying to fell trees with a blunt instrument.

Courageous followers will work long and hard to forward the common purpose when necessary, but also need to organize their work so the output is timely and the pace is sustainable.

TAKING CARE OF OURSELVES

Management of our life and health are even more fundamental than management of our work if we are to be reliable team members and a source of support for our leaders. The more passionately we feel about a leader or cause the more we are at risk of not taking care of ourselves, sacrificing our health, or damaging our personal relations. There is always another urgent matter to attend to, something that will make a difference.

We must do our jobs, not become our jobs. A follower may feel heroic working fifteen-hour days or ninety-hour weeks. Sometimes we feel pressured into long hours by the example the leader is setting. Occasionally, we do need to work this hard for short periods of time. But if excessive time at work becomes a long-standing pattern, we must change it before it depletes our energy and wreaks havoc in other parts of our lives.

If we do not assume responsibility for getting the nurturing we need as human beings, we will burn out sooner or later. In doing so, we often let down the people we are serving, sometimes very unpleasantly. To serve well we must be passionately committed to our jobs, but not be consumed by that passion.

Ideally, we will find the right balance between work and other parts of our lives. Sometimes we don't manage to do this. We begin to burn out. There are telltale signs: exhaustion, chronic frustration, shortness of temper, frayed relations, feelings of emptiness, lack of caring, wanting to be elsewhere.

We need to stay alert to these signs and periodically examine the balance we are striking:

What areas of our life need attention?

What must be changed to allow us to give that attention?

Are negotiations with the leader needed to make these changes?

Is the relationship with the leader healthy enough to comfortably conduct these negotiations?

Does the leader-follower relationship itself need to be renegotiated?

What are the respective needs that must be balanced for the negotiations to be successful?

Managing our life and health is not a marginal issue. In the long run it can make the difference between brilliantly contributing to the common purpose and blowing up or fizzling out in the attempt.

PASSION

Successful followers care passionately about their work and the people it serves. They have a sense of ownership, of stewardship. If something happens, it is happening to what they are responsible for. When followers and leaders share a passion for the work, they can be full partners in it. Unless we match a leader's passion, it is difficult to become more than a junior partner.

We can be passionate for the overall work and also for whatever role we have within it. When the clerk in charge of a supply room or publications stock maintains a beautifully organized facility that smoothly supports the rest of the organization, professional pride shines through. Appreciating the uniqueness of a role and its impact permits us to imbue the role with the energy needed to multiply our contribution.

Passion cannot be manufactured or faked. It springs from genuine connection to the common purpose. It may be clouded by setbacks to that purpose, but is always available to be retapped. Courageous followers are not content to accept a loss of passion as "normal." They ask themselves and others tough questions that can reignite passion:

Does the organization's sense of purpose need renewing?

Have we personally lost touch with the shared purpose and vision of the organization?

What is our own vision of fulfillment?

How does our current role allow us to achieve this?

How does our current role position us to achieve even greater fulfillment in the future?

Are frustrations in accomplishing our current role blocking our passion?

Are relationship issues with the leader or other group members blocking our passion?

Are we ready for more responsibility and do we need to make this readiness known?

Restoring passion reconnects us with our power. Without passion we cannot excel. By excelling we fulfill ourselves and earn the right to help shape the organization's future. Armchair critics have little influence with the leader and group whereas team members passionately fulfilling their role can weigh in heavily.

INITIATIVE

Willingness to initiate action without being instructed to do so is a distinguishing characteristic of the courageous follower. Courageous followers assume responsibility for events in their vicinity—whether it be a customer service complaint or an opportunity that, if seized, can produce a quantum leap forward for the organization.

If we are to strengthen our capacity to initiate it may help to bear in mind these factors:

As courageous followers, we view ourselves as full participants committed to shared values and a common purpose. We are not spectators; we don't just watch, we act.

When a common purpose guides both the leader and follower, control shifts from the leader to the purpose itself; we don't require permission to act in ways that forward the purpose.

If we understand the organization's purpose, we can initiate fresh ways to communicate that purpose and to pursue it.

We need to keep sufficiently informed to understand the context and nuances of events so we can initiate responses to unexpected threats and opportunities with confidence and judgment.

It is our responsibility to understand what risks are acceptable for the organization and what risks are unacceptable.

It is a failure of responsibility not to act when the risks are acceptable and the purpose and values of the group would have us act.

It is a failure of responsibility to act when the risks are unacceptable and acting endangers the organization's purpose or violates its values.

Leaders usually support acts of initiative unless followers appear to be redirecting the spotlight to themselves at the leader's expense. If the initiative is motivated by service to the common purpose and not self-aggrandizement, leaders are prone to treat it with collegial respect—the follower is sharing the responsibilities of leadership.

INFLUENCING THE CULTURE

Every group has a distinctive culture: a set of norms for behaving and a way of looking at the world. Successful leaders and followers must learn the norms and respect the power of an existing culture. The stories of political appointees disregarding the culture of a bureaucracy and then being defeated by it are legion. But our universe and our cultures are interactive; a follower is not walking a one-way street. A courageous follower who respects a culture can also influence it.

Too often, a follower's instinct is to blend in and adapt to the attitudes of a group even if they are passive, cynical, or defeatist. Courageous followers don't allow their own values to be subsumed by the prevailing culture. We can influence the existing culture if we respect these principles:

Our willingness to stand out, to demonstrate differing attitudes, not as a challenge to the group but simply as an expression of our own outlook and vision, adds strength to the organization.

Our appreciation and support of the values and traditions that give group pride and cohesion allow us to credibly model other characteristics not currently embraced by the group.

By staying true to our own values and vision and linking these to the common purpose, we can influence the energy the group generates for accomplishing the purpose.

Adhering to our own "higher" inclinations in a culture that doesn't obviously support them requires clarity of values and self-acceptance.

A follower's ability to remain his own person while bonding with the group is the same ability that allows a follower to challenge the group or its leaders when the need to do so arises. Followers who successfully influence a group by modeling other behaviors in a nonconfrontational mode establish their integrity and earn the group's respect. They are in a strong position to challenge the group if that is needed at a future point.

BREAKING THE RULES

Effective followers assume responsibility for learning the rules of the system in which they operate. Rules are created as guidelines for using the group's resources, as methods for orderly decision making, as assurances of fairness, as clarification and guarantees of expected standards. Rules are the agreements by which the group maintains its identity, expresses its values, and coordinates its activities. An effective follower understands the rules and knows how to get things done within their framework.

Courageous followers also recognize the subordinate relationship of rules to purpose. They are alert to the evolution or interpretation of rules that may impede the accomplishment of the organization's purpose. They have an adult understanding of rules: they support rules when they serve the common purpose and question rules when they thwart the purpose.

Often, if we trace down the source of a rule that seems to violate common sense and obstruct service, we find it is being applied in a way that was never intended. Rules usually evolve in an historical context and, as the context changes, rules need to be reviewed for relevancy. Nothing more quickly tests our patience as customers than an employee telling us we can't do something that common sense demands be done. We sometimes wonder what is happening to the hundreds of millions of dollars spent on customer service programs when we encounter an employee obstinately insisting on "company policy."

Our attitude toward rules is critical. It affects our relationship to the leader and our response to the leader when questionable orders are issued. The following guidelines may help when we are confronted with rules that seem to thwart the organization's purpose or clash with its values:

> **It is not ethical to break rules for simple convenience or for personal gain, but neither is it ethical to comply with or enforce rules if they impede the accomplishment of the organization's purpose, the organization's values, or basic human decency.**

> **A courageous follower assumes responsibility in dilemmas where rules impede service and is willing to bend, circumvent, or break the rules to get things done.**

> **When a rule impedes an organization's ability to give appropriate service, courageous followers do not hide their circumvention but use it as an example of why the rule must be vigorously reviewed.**

> **Followers who find themselves hiding their circumvention of rules should carefully examine their motivations and assumptions. This type of deception is inappropriate in all but the most repressive of climates.**

Courageous followers trust themselves, and are trusted by the organization, to be interpreters of the organization's values when applying a rule to a specific circumstance. Occasionally, at senior levels of government or private industry, we see individuals using the discretion entrusted to them to justify criminal acts. This, of course, is not an act of courage but a betrayal of the trust placed in them by the organization's stakeholders.

BREAKING THE MINDSET

Sometimes, it is not just rules that need to be broken but the organization's whole mindset. The pursuit of the common purpose may be hampered by the group's assumptions about the world. These assumptions are lenses through which the group filters information. Sometimes, the lenses also filter out important possibilities.

It is a great challenge to help a group escape the limits of its current mindset; we are asking the group to make a leap into territory it doesn't even realize exists. Courageous followers who wish to present a new paradigm must carefully prepare the group to receive it, or they will be met with blank stares and quick rejections. The group doesn't have a framework on which to register and evaluate the ideas. For example, an organization that hasn't begun grappling with its lack of cultural diversity has no inkling of the real issues, let alone how they themselves contribute to the problem.

We must be willing to take our concerns about the organization's current paradigm to the highest level of leadership and begin creating awareness there of the issues. We need to prepare our resources well for creating this awareness and an awareness of alternative paradigms. These resources might include:

> statistics—the numerical facts about a group's current practice,
>
> case histories and anecdotes,
>
> comparison with other groups' practices,
>
> outside experts and studies,
>
> impact statements from affected stakeholders,
>
> historical analogies,
>
> tours and inspections of widely different models,
>
> future scenarios of the extension of current practices.

Once awareness is created, a courageous follower can enlist the group's energy to begin exploring new possibilities.

IMPROVING PROCESSES

Processes are the chains of activity through which an organization fulfills its needs and the needs of the individuals and groups with which it interacts. Core processes are what permit the organization to achieve its purpose, and other processes support these.

One danger in a group is that each member vaguely thinks someone else should do something about flaws they observe in its processes. Frequently, group members see inefficiencies but don't act on ideas they have for remedying them. Failure to act lowers a follower's sense of responsibility for what is occurring. Each follower thinks, "If I were in charge, I would do it differently, but I'm not in charge, so it's not my problem." Meanwhile, the common purpose suffers.

Courageous followers do not quietly ignore or ineffectively complain about wrongs they see. They do not assume that others also see these things and will correct them. They look for and find the avenues open to them for effecting change.

When considering responsibilities for the organization's processes, bear in mind these thoughts:

> **Remedying a specific service complaint helps retain the individual customer's loyalty, but remedying the process that caused it saves the loyalty of many.**
>
> **If there is a clear process owner who has official responsibility for that process, our minimum responsibility is to ensure that the owner is aware of the process flaws we have observed.**
>
> **If there is no clear process owner or process improvement team, we should alert the organization to the need for one.**
>
> **Courageous followers don't just tell the leader "something should be done about this," adding to the burden of leadership, but present ideas for improving the process that the leader can consider.**

Improving a process, such as the fulfillment of member requests in an association, the involvement of community groups in policy making, or the shortening of response time to customer orders, often requires a champion to focus the organization on the need for it and to ensure that the necessary follow-through occurs. A courageous follower is willing to be this champion.

TESTING YOUR IDEAS

Sometimes an organization isn't ready to address a deficiency or try a better way of doing things. Other needs seem more pressing. This can be frustrating to a follower who feels strongly about an issue. Throwing up our hands and giving up is not assuming responsibility. Our challenge is to find a way to test our ideas by putting them into action and demonstrating their potential. With determination and creativity, new processes and approaches can usually be piloted without a prohibitive expenditure of resources. Designing a pilot that can be conducted out of an existing budget simplifies or eliminates the initial approval process.

In addition to designing a sound pilot with good measurements, we need to pay attention to how we will build consensus for the idea if the pilot is successful. Our chances for gaining acceptance of the idea improve if we secure the early involvement of people whose opinion decision makers value. They will help us take our idea from the successful pilot stage to implementation.

If we are successful, we must remember to give plenty of credit to those who supported the pilot and to the leader who tacitly let us conduct it. If the idea flops, we learn from it and move on to the next idea. When we put our ideas on the line by testing them, we risk failure. When followers initiate and take risks, there is a healthy blurring of the line between followership and leadership.

3

THE COURAGE
TO SERVE

 I NEVER CEASE TO BE AMAZED at how many decisions a good chief of staff makes for a U.S. senator without consultation. Given the hundreds of small and large requests a senator receives daily, this is an essential function. It is also the epitome of judgment in serving a leader: knowing when you can speak for the leader and when you had better consult her. It takes courage to serve as a close aide to a senior leader. If you bother leaders with too many matters, you will squander their energy; if you fail to bring things that they need to know to their attention, you may blindside them, causing embarrassment or calamity.

In many organizational cultures, when things go wrong someone has to pay, to be offered up as a sacrifice, and it may be you. In the British and other governments, it is customary for a minister to resign if there's been a scandal that could tar the prime minister. Like chess, the bishops and rooks are offered to save the king.

At the same time, you may never get all of the credit for the hard work you do. Some of it is done in the leader's name and it is she who presents the ideas to the board or the press. Yet if the leader falls from favor, as a close aide you may go down with her.

Some people prefer a safe backwater in the organization, and you can hardly blame them. Those closest to a leader often live with a high level of stress. One senator, who retained a consulting group I directed, has very high standards and equally volatile emotions. A minivan driver, who had been hired for the day to take the senator and some of his staff to a string of speaking engagements, listened as the senator repeatedly upbraided his staff about various details. "I get it!" the driver said to one of the staff who stayed behind during one speech. "You put up with this because they pay you a million dollars a year!" It was the only way he could imagine anyone would voluntarily put up with that kind of stress.

There is art to serving a dynamic leader. Done well, with superior skill, both our stress level and the leader's can be kept down and creative energy can be maximized. Brilliant support contributes as much to an organization's ability to fulfill its purpose as does brilliant leadership. Too often, I've seen leaders grow increasingly overworked, frustrated, and ill-tempered. They haven't known how to get the support they need. Whether the leader asks for it or not, followers need to give the leader the support she needs and help her if she doesn't know how to accept it.

Serving a leader is a complex task. It demands a high degree of organizational know-how. It requires helping the leader manage time and information. It calls for vigorously projecting the leader's values and message. It asks for great judgment, even wisdom. And it can necessitate being very cool under fire.

CONSERVING A LEADER'S ENERGY

Leaders occupy positions of high visibility and are often buffeted by powerful forces. Internal and external pressures build and can test or distort a leader's values and judgment. An important function of followership is minimizing unnecessary pressure that may contribute to this distortion.

Courageous followers help leaders make choices about demands that push their personal and professional lives out of balance. Leaders are often driven personalities; they use their bountiful energy to inspire or cajole the organization to fulfill its purpose. But this bountiful energy isn't boundless, even if the leader thinks it is. It must be conserved and renewed. Questions we should ask and consider include:

What kinds of activities refresh the leader?

Is there sufficient time scheduled for these activities and is it vigorously defended?

> What activities take the greatest toll on the leader's creativity and temperament?

> How can energy-draining activities be minimized or prepared for in ways that reduce the toll they take?

> How can we organize to permit the leader to focus more on high-payback activities?

> What functions has the leader always done that should now be delegated?

> What activities are central to the leader's role and should not be delegated, but should be better supported?

If internal pressure is driving the leader to do "too much," we must confront her with the consequences. If the leader is micromanaging we must challenge her to trust more. With a micromanager, we should avoid slipping into a pattern of not attending to the details of our work "because the leader will change it anyway." This reinforces a leader's belief that she has to "do everything" and contributes to the downward spiral of overload and fatigue.

The courageous follower is willing to both comfort and confront the leader, to assume additional responsibilities to relieve the leader, or to initiate dialogue to help the leader examine her own contribution to the overload.

ORGANIZING COMMUNICATION PROCESSES

Appropriate organization is necessary to achieve the common purpose and to support the leader. From the most complex society right down to the individual cell, all life must organize itself. Higher life organizes itself around a vision, values, and goals. Effective followers help leaders clarify the vision and goals and develop the organization that the group needs to pursue them.

The most important organizational structures and processes are those concerning communication. They tell us how all other organizational processes are functioning. A survey of almost any organization shows that few leaders organize communication processes that are fully satisfactory to the group. To serve a leader well, we must help the leader detect communication deficiencies and design the right combination of communication vehicles to satisfy the organization's needs. The design of communication processes should be sensitive to multiple needs, including the need for:

the leader to communicate her vision directly to all levels of the organization and its stakeholders;

stakeholders to be able to communicate their views to the leader;

mechanisms to summarize communication to a leader and help her prepare responses so she is not overwhelmed by volume;

information to move swiftly up, down, across, in, and out of the organization so no parts of the group or its environment are left unconnected;

information to circulate among all members of natural work groups so that class distinctions aren't created or reinforced;

information to be freely circulated, but not overcirculated so that it jams an organization's functioning or compromises its competitiveness;

the right combination of media and technologies to facilitate communication in an array of situations;

communication that leads to creativity, distributed decision making, coordination, implementation, and evaluation.

Continuous review is required to achieve balance in a communication system so that all levels are touched in a timely way, in all directions, without overburdening the leader or the organization.

ACQUIRING ACCESS

Obtaining the right amount of access to a leader requires striking a delicate balance. Followers must have or negotiate a certain degree of access to support a leader and perform their roles. But followers often desire more access than a leader can realistically give or than they necessarily need. We must be alert to our own ego-based desire for unnecessary access and keep this in balance so it does not put undue strain on a leader's time and energy. However, we should not allow our exaggerated sense of a leader's importance and time constraints to keep us from requesting access when it is appropriate for accomplishing critical tasks or building and maintaining our relationship.

We can bear in mind these guidelines for improving our access:

> If we genuinely require more access we must make whatever access we already enjoy valuable to the leader.

> We must know our own communication weaknesses, such as rambling or getting too technical, that diminish a leader's willingness to grant needed access, and work to keep these weaknesses in check.

> Focusing on high-value issues and being well prepared are a base line for improved access, but are not necessarily sufficient.

> Relaxed but productive and stimulating interchange may recharge a leader in ways that formal meetings don't, causing the leader to seek out more contact with us.

> Candor can create further receptivity in a leader as it is too often lacking in the atmosphere surrounding prominent leaders.

> We should be aware of how the leader best receives and processes information and stress that vehicle—oral, written, electronic, graphic, experiential—to maximize the value of the access we do have.

Courageous followers empower themselves so they don't require excessive access to make decisions. Empowerment requires internal confidence and external assumption or negotiation of authority to support the common purpose. A robust relationship with the leader is needed to fulfill the potential of the follower's role. Appropriate access is both a requirement and sign of that relationship.

THE RESPONSIBILITIES OF GATEKEEPING

Followers who control the access of other followers to a leader have the responsibility to use this power fairly. The power of proximity to power is itself intoxicating and can inflate egos. Gatekeepers need to guard against becoming arrogant and indifferent to the needs of those seeking access to the leader. If supporting a leader requires blocking or limiting access to an overloaded leader, a gatekeeper can do so with empathy and find other ways to help the person seeking access. A gatekeeper can become less a border guard and more of a traveler's aid station—a traffic router, networker, and facilitator.

Gatekeepers should not allow their own prejudices to insulate the leader from competing views or disapproved of sources. We must guard against litmus tests or subtle cultural biases, which limit the diversity of ideas reaching a leader. A gatekeeper must also avoid biasing a leader's receptivity to a communication by introducing it derogatorily: "Oh, here's *another* memo from so and so." Biased remarks by a gatekeeper are a form of pandering to a leader's perceived prejudices, or imposing one's own.

A gatekeeper who distorts the screening process or abuses the leader's reflected power hurts the leader and the organization. A courageous follower confronts this issue head on with the gatekeeper and, as necessary, with the leader. A functional gatekeeper protects those within the walls but freely lets in the commerce of ideas that keeps the community vibrant. A dysfunctional gatekeeper just keeps slamming doors.

Prominent leaders often receive many requests to lend their prestige to causes and events—charities, boards, coalitions, political activities, symposiums, civic initiatives. If leaders overcommit they become distracted from the common purpose. Effective followers do not necessarily leave this larger gatekeeping process to one individual. They establish a process to insulate an in-demand leader from excessive pressure and help her make balanced choices about which invitations to accept, delegate, or decline. A schedule reflects a leader's values and priorities, and the process for developing it should not be taken lightly.

Competing scheduling requests can be batched and evaluated against well-thought-out criteria by a small, functionally balanced group. Some possible criteria are:

> **What opportunity does this invitation present for advancing the organization's purpose?**
>
> **What message does accepting or declining send about the leader's values?**
>
> **What is competing with this opportunity for the leader's time and what value does that have to the organization?**
>
> **Can the request be meaningfully delegated?**

A well-thought-out scheduling process helps the leader and organization stay focused on the common purpose and the strategy for achieving it.

BUFFERING A LEADER

Great leaders face great challenges. They often encounter relentless opposition while seeking a path that will achieve their organization's purpose. Read the biographies of Winston Churchill, Martin Luther King, Jr., or Ghandi and you will find years of patience-wearing struggle and setbacks. Many less famous leaders also labor for years or decades before they see their dreams materialize.

We must take great care not to compound the real external challenges by relaying bad information and unsubstantiated rumors to a leader. These create an exaggerated perception of external pressure or hostility to which an inflamed leader may overreact. A follower who is in the habit of running to a leader with unsubstantiated rumors and gossip is serving some personal psychological need rather than the leader.

When confronted with alarming "news" for the leader we might ask ourselves:

> **What do we actually know versus what have we been told?**
>
> **Does it make sense or do we need to corroborate it further?**
>
> **Do we have both the facts and the context in which they occurred?**
>
> **If an event actually occurred, what's behind it?**
>
> **Should we accept the events at face value or explore if they have been manipulated to serve another agenda into which we are being drawn?**
>
> **Is the information we have sufficient or do we need to gather further information so we can make recommendations?**

Once information has been substantiated, we should never protect a leader from bad news as it is an important source of feedback. When reporting bad news, we should attempt to provide the leader with options that support the group's value system as this will be a time when values are tested:

> **"This is what has occurred and here are three options we've developed."**
>
> **"The most expedient course is _____ but it doesn't serve our values and purpose well in the long run, so we recommend _____ ."**

A steady stream of bad news may demoralize the leader and sap the will required to carry on. To balance the picture we need to also present examples of how the leader's efforts and commitment to the common purpose are successful. Even small successes can sustain an embattled leader and group in their struggle.

DEFENDING THE LEADER

It is easy for people inside or outside of the organization to target a leader because the leader is visible and represents the organization and its authority. Sometimes there is a lot of behind-the-back complaining about a leader. While the complaints may be legitimate, this form of addressing them is not. It creates an atmosphere of diminished mutual respect, increased alienation, and lackluster implementation of strategy. When we encounter it we need to defend our leaders.

It is important for a group to remember its leader's strengths, which sometimes are forgotten or taken for granted. Whatever flaws a leader may have, her strengths may be holding the organization together or contributing significantly to the organization's purpose. A courageous follower who encounters chronic complaining challenges the group to remember the leader's strengths. We can only give constructive feedback from a perspective of true regard for the individual.

If we are among the complainers, a hard examination of our own role may be in order. Complaining may be a way of projecting onto the leader our frustration at not being more successful in our efforts. We need to examine how we can assume more responsibility and be more effective.

Complaining should not be ignored or repressed. There is something to learn from it. The courageous follower urges complainers to package and deliver their communications in useful ways rather than filling the airwaves with discontent.

BUFFERING OTHERS FROM A LEADER

There is often such deference paid to authority that the slightest comment made by a leader is taken literally. Leaders can be mortified to find an off-the-cuff comment they made was construed to be "policy," a one-time solution to a unique situation was interpreted as a change in standard procedure, or an angry reaction was conveyed as their final position. If an instruction from a leader seems to fly in the face of good sense, a follower at any level should request clarification before implementing it. This seems to be such common sense as to not deserve mention, but the principle is often violated by followers who have not yet found their own locus of responsibility.

If we work as a close aide to a leader we have a special role to play in relaying communication from the leader. We must sometimes function as a step-down transformer, taking a high voltage emanation from the leader and modulating it so it can be received usefully at its intended receipt point several levels down an organization. The leader would do the same if she were talking to people she only sees occasionally. Just as we often address new acquaintances with more circumspection than we do intimate friends, the different levels of comfort and familiarity some people have with the leader demand judgment in how we relay a leader's thoughts, feelings, and instructions. When we find ourselves in this facilitative role, these guidelines may help:

A leader's message should not be diluted, but it is our responsibility to understand the context in which it was delivered and how this differs from the context in which it will be received.

Facilitation may require faithfully interpreting and relaying the essential communication while modifying the quality of the carrier wave so that it can be received as intended.

It is our responsibility to help others understand what the leader is communicating, and to detect and clarify false impressions that may block acceptance or implementation.

Literally relaying or thoughtlessly implementing all of a leader's instructions is not true support, but an effective way of undoing a leader.

ACTING IN THE LEADER'S NAME

When we are a close aide to a leader, our acts are often perceived as extensions of the leader's values and intentions. In organizations in which the leader is focused on strategic and external priorities, we may become the primary contact point for the rest of the organization and exert great influence on it. Intentionally or not, we can create an atmosphere that doesn't reflect the leader's values.

Acting in the leader's name is a delicate affair. Yet we must be willing to do it. We need a high degree of awareness of how our tone and actions support or detract from the leader's values. If we allow our own issues with power to reflect poorly on the leader we may do serious damage to the organization and, eventually, to our career. For example, if we are more prone to a rigid command-and-control style of management than the leader, and staff want the organization to be more participatory, we may generate strong resentment toward "management." When the leader becomes aware of how this is weakening the group's commitment to the common purpose, she may need to dramatically distance herself from us.

By staying closely attuned to the leader we can reflect her values and approve or initiate actions that are consistent with those values and goals without burdening the leader with details. Clarifying in advance the categories of decisions we will make can prevent overstepping our authority. We might ask ourselves these questions when considering if we can speak for the leader in specific situations:

What has the leader's position been on similar issues in the past?

Has the leader recently expressed clear feelings on this issue?

Is the leader in the process of reviewing her position on this issue?

Am I comfortable with what I perceive to be the leader's position on this?

Is there anything that makes this a special case warranting consultation?

We must be careful not to interject our own agendas in the leader's name. When courageous followers feel strongly about an issue and the leader does not, they take a stand on that issue in their own name and do not infer the leader's support for it. They appreciate the power conferred on them and do not abuse it by blurring the boundaries between themselves and the leader.

DEFINING A LEADER PUBLICLY

In many activities, an organization's supporters and adversaries form their opinion of the organization from the perception they have of its leaders. If the leader has an image that commands attention and respect, the organization is in a stronger position to achieve its purpose.

An effective organization does not wait for those outside the organization to define its leader's image. Outsiders often do so in light of their own agendas or based on isolated experiences. It is better to publicly define our own leaders in terms of their real strengths, values, achievements, and goals. At lower levels of leadership this may be as simple as mentioning these when we speak to more senior leaders or to leaders of other groups. At higher levels this may warrant an orchestrated public relations effort. Successful public relations uses only images built on reality. It is the leader's responsibility to live by the values she projects. It is our responsibility to help her do this.

We must not expect perfection from our leaders as this contributes to the delusion of the infallible leader. We are right to expect, however, that leaders substantively live up to the image we are projecting with their agreement. By confronting leaders about departures from their publicly stated values, we help them remain the people they want to be.

There are several principles to keep in mind when projecting a leader's image:

> We should never cover up a leader's behavior that does not conform to her public image.

> We should use the discrepancy between publicly held values and personal behavior as feedback to help a leader reexamine her values and behavior.

> Simultaneously, we should act to prevent the leader's detractors from redefining her image based on behavior that was an exception to her values and virtues.

Reducing the complexity of a human being to digestible images is dangerous and difficult, but courageous followers recognize that this occurs and participate in the process with a deep regard for truth.

FOCUSING THE CREATIVE LEADER

A creative leader is a fount of ideas. This is of great value to an organization. But if followers attempt to indiscriminately implement all of a prolific leader's ideas, focus will be lost and the leader and organization may become exhausted.

If the leader's ideas completely fill the group's agenda there will be no room for followers to contribute their own creativity. It is a critical function of courageous followership to evaluate the flow of ideas from a leader and to determine which have the greatest potential for forwarding the common purpose. Criteria should be established for evaluating ideas and opportunities. The criteria may include:

> Does this idea forward our core mission?

> How large is the potential payoff for our stakeholders?

> Will it drain resources from higher payoff activities?

Does it make the best use of our strengths and talents?

Will it leave us in a stronger position to fulfill our purpose?

Does it have serious downsides or entail unacceptable risks?

A process is needed to select the ideas that are real gems. We should energetically implement these and demonstrate to the leader how implementing the numerous other ideas will detract from the gems. If the leader is usually respectful of the evaluation process, but convinced a particular idea should be pursued despite the tradeoffs, courageous followers support her unless the risks are overwhelming. Creative intuition cannot always be subordinated to analytical processes.

PRESENTING OPTIONS

Even the most creative leaders appreciate it when others present them with options for handling situations. The options followers generate often circumscribe the range of actions a leader contemplates. The quality of those options makes a huge difference to the success of an organization. Neither we nor our leaders should settle for good ideas on important issues until we have energetically searched for great ideas.

Before we can present options we need to be sure we are solving the right problem. What seems like an isolated problem is often one manifestation of a complex set of interactions within a system. We need to search for the questions that will unearth the fundamental problem instead of searching for solutions to the apparent problem. We can learn different systems for doing this, such as the Ishikawa cause-and-effect "fishbone diagram," or Kepner/Tregoe's situation-and-problem-analysis processes, or Stephen Brookfield's critical-thinking approach.

The courageous follower at times sounds like a philosopher:

What do we think we know?

Why do we think we know this?

What assumptions underlie our belief?

Under what circumstances are these assumptions valid?

Do the current circumstances approximate these?

How are they different?

What successful examples are there of operating on those assumptions?

What unsuccessful examples are there?

What can we learn from these examples?

Is there an entirely different way to think about this?

Is there something we can learn from thinking in a new way?

Can we draw analogies from unrelated fields that will further unlock our thinking?

In the best of worlds the leader and group are open to this type of process. If they are not, we can ask these questions of ourselves and inject our answers into whatever dialogue exists.

What seems like the cause of a problem is often just the effect of a deeper problem. We can use the "rule of three whys" to get at the root of a problem, successively asking why something is so until a fundamental reason is uncovered:

Why is this so? Answer.

Why would that be so? Answer.

Why would that be the case? Answer.

The need to identify the right problem must be balanced by the need to avoid "analysis paralysis." Leadership requires making difficult decisions with incomplete data. The time comes for the follower to cease asking questions and to present concrete options. Depending on the urgency of the situation this may occur in minutes or in months. Integrity is then served by following the "rule of three options."

Develop at least three good options for any situation.

By presenting several workable options, we give leaders genuine choices, not just the choices we want them to make.

If one choice presents ethical problems, we are less tempted to ignore the problems if we have other options.

The pros and cons of each option can be weighed, the benefits and dangers evaluated, and the best option or synthesis of options selected. Courageous followers help their leaders go beyond popular wisdom and search for fundamental understanding of issues, from which visionary leadership can develop.

KNOWING WHEN YOU DON'T KNOW

Followers can experience enormous psychological pressure to look good around a leader and provide answers to questions "off the cuff." Our culture values the expert who can spout off opinions more than the sage who contemplates.

Courageous followers regard the act of advising as a trust. They differentiate between what they know factually, what they intuit, and what they don't know at all. They don't overstate their case.

"I've researched this and can tell you unequivocally that _____ ."

"I've met with them and know they feel strongly about that so I advise against doing it."

"All I can tell you is what my gut says."

"My feeling is to go with _____ but I'd want to run it through a full decision-making process."

"I don't have a clear sense about that—let me think about it and get back to you."

"That's not my area of experience. Have you consulted _____ who has worked a lot with that?"

If we are close to a leader we can serve as a sounding board, reflecting back what we hear without pretending expertise we lack:

"You sound uncomfortable with that idea. Are you?"

"From what I know of you, you tend to be cautious. Are you being overly cautious in this situation?"

"My sense is that you can trust him. Is there anything making you feel otherwise?"

"From what I've heard you say, your confidence seems justified."

"There's something that doesn't ring true. Can you clarify the situation a bit more?"

In this way we can help a leader think through difficult issues or prepare for critical events despite our lack of expertise on a particular subject. Courageous followers are confident enough of their value to the leader that they do not need to inflate that value with pretended expertise.

AVOIDING INSULARITY

There is a danger that the very success of the leader-follower relationship may weaken a leader. Leaders who become comfortable with their closest followers may begin to rely only on them for information, counsel, and feedback. Insularity occurs, and both leader and followers lose perspective and freshness of ideas; the team grows stale. If we always see the same kind of people, we always have the same kind of ideas.

Many newly elected presidents of the United States surround themselves with lifelong friends. Each has his equivalent of Jimmy Carter's

"Georgia mafia." The impulse is understandable. Taken too far, however, it is dangerous and works against a leader. We are prone to surround ourselves with people whose experiences, ideas, and temperaments are compatible with ours. They are mirrors, albeit mirrors set at different angles. Mirrors are important, but in different situations we need a variety of optical devices to perceive and understand events: microscopes, telescopes, periscopes, spectroscopes, infrared night-vision equipment. Relying on one type of instrument permits us to see what that instrument is good at seeing. To use power well, we must see and understand events from many perspectives, at many levels.

As close aides, consciously or not, we may encourage the tendency of leaders to narrow their sources of counsel because this increases our own power. Our egos nudge the common purpose off center stage. It takes courage to welcome others, who may dilute our power, into the inner circle. By bearing in mind the following observations and guidelines, we may avoid complicity in the tendency to insularity:

> All humans long for greater power over their destiny; by serving a powerful leader who comes to rely on us, we feel more in control of our destiny.

> In our desire for our leader to be powerful and for ourselves to remain close to this power, we can blind ourselves to a leader's flaws and lose our ability to effectively provide feedback.

> Though it goes against our instinct for accruing power to ourselves, we must encourage a leader to periodically seek other perspectives without the filter of close followers.

> If we insulate the leader and ourselves from other perspectives, there is a far greater chance we will misuse and lose the power we desire.

Other perspectives provide a reality check on the relationship of a leader and close followers. Once followers move past feeling threatened, they too learn from the new perspectives; they too gain access to new ways of seeing. Diversity is a primary source of the balance needed to use power wisely.

ENCOURAGING PEER RELATIONS

No matter how healthy the relationship between a leader and followers, it is not a substitute for a leader's relationships with peers. Even in a relaxed leader-follower relationship there is always some tendency to maintain a little distance, a distinction in roles. We need to be alert to a leader who lacks peer relationships and encourage their development. Men, in particular, are not known for tending to their relationships. Sometimes as they move up the ladder they leave friends behind and wind up instead with associates.

Some leaders mix in their professional circles. While important, this tends to be a business or political activity. They are presenting their social personae. Leaders need relationships that get below the surface, relationships that allow them to talk about their vulnerabilities as well as their strengths.

The need for peer relations exists for all leaders, but is critical for charismatic leaders such as religious figures whose followers' devotion blinds them to their flaws. We have seen the number of evangelical ministers who have fallen from grace in recent years. Courageous followers must encourage charismatic leaders to cultivate relationships with others who do not hold them in awe.

It may require someone who has known the leader in different roles and stages of development to "get through" to him. It may require someone of similar stature to empathize with and challenge him. He may just need a buddy to have a heart-to-heart talk with. A close relationship with just one peer can also present a problem, however, if the relationship mutually reinforces an unhealthy condition such as sexism or alcoholism. A diversity of peer relationships avoids undue influence by one individual. Peer relationships might include:

a longtime friend or relative,

other prominent leaders in the same or related fields,

a former follower who has become a leader of comparable stature,

a former mentor who reestablishes a relationship with the leader,

a peer support group, such as a monthly roundtable in which business leaders discuss their problems,

a spiritual counselor, respected author, or consultant who can speak to a leader on equal terms.

It is not the role of followers to engineer a leader's social relations. But it is the role of courageous followers to stay alert to a leader's well-being. Isolation from peers is a warning sign that should be heeded.

MANAGING CRISES

We often hear that a leader's job in a crisis is to keep the environment calm enough so that people can get their work done. Followers also have this responsibility—to be productive and supportive while a path is charted through the crisis. Often, events unfold too rapidly for a leader and followers to fully consult with each other before acting. Trust and morale can be strengthened or shattered depending on responses made in these trying conditions.

Crisis preparation is a key tool in crisis management. For example, we can determine likely scenarios in which the leader or followers may need to make important decisions. Then we can develop and record guidelines for emergency responses which adhere to our values. In addition, in an acute crisis, we must be prepared to give the leader or acting leader complete support. In a rapidly unfolding situation, we may need to suspend our responsibility to fully understand what we are being asked to do before we act. This itself is an act of courage.

If normal decision-support processes are suspended, it is important that the group reassert these at the earliest possible moment. We must be careful the curtailed consultation demanded by an emergency response doesn't become a new norm due to recurring crises. Recurring crises are a glaring sign of poor management, which must be analyzed and remedied.

There is a distinction between recurring crises and a prolonged crisis. A prolonged crisis, such as one stemming from a faulty product and the years of litigation and adverse publicity it generates, may reflect a specific management error that has long since been corrected. Nevertheless, the duration of the fallout from the error may erode the leader's and group's morale through constant buffeting. The instinct for self-preservation may well up and threaten to pull apart the organization. If stress has attenuated the leader's capacity for facing the public and rallying the organization, we may have to compensate for the leader.

Our actions to support the leader and hold the organization together should include:

> reaffirming the group's sense of purpose as a context in which to absorb the crisis;

> unburdening the leader of usual or extra duties if the emotional stress of the crisis is threatening the leader's ability to function;

> keeping the group fully and honestly briefed on actual and anticipated developments to reduce rumors and shocks;

> isolating the contact points in the organization to those designated and trained to specifically deal with the crisis, so the rest can get their work done;

> using the crisis to spur self-examination by the organization so that reforms to address underlying causes can be initiated;

> helping the group, after the acute phase of the crisis has passed, to process any trauma.

If we assumed leadership prerogatives during a crisis we should be attentive to relinquishing them when the crisis is over unless our formal authority has been expanded. Failure to do this can generate confusion and mistrust. An organization that manages a crisis well strengthens the bonds between leaders and followers. An organization that doesn't, may simply form painful scar tissue.

WHEN THE LEADER IS ILL

The stress of leadership is high. It takes a physical as well as psychological toll. Drug or alcohol addiction is particularly problematic, but ulcers, hypertension, or migraine headaches can also interfere with a leader's performance or be aggravated by pressures on the leader. Different types of illness have different durations and complications. Each poses its own challenge to followers, from a six-week bout with Lyme disease to a survived heart attack, a battle with cancer, or progressive dementia.

Though serious illness can strike at any age, it is more common as people grow older. Senior leadership positions tend to be filled with older, more experienced people. Thus, illness among leaders is more common than we think. A close follower is faced with a special type of crisis when the leader is ill. The support a leader needs can become more demanding and pose new problems.

In lower levels of leadership, the challenge is often how to keep things going in the leader's absence or unburden her sufficiently so she can get the rest needed to recover. As in a crisis, we must decide what responsibility and authority is appropriate for us to assume.

In higher levels of leadership, the problem can become complicated because the attending physician may also be a follower who is balancing medical and business or political priorities. A head of state always has a personal physician. Often, so do other senior ranking officials, celebrities, or wealthy industrialists. Sometimes there is great pressure on the physicians and the inner circle to collude in masking a medical condition from the public. It can be extremely dangerous to allow leaders to make high-level decisions, perform critical negotiations, or engage in taxing events when their physical and mental processes are impaired by illness, pain, or medication. In its final years, the former Soviet Union was plagued with this condition in its leaders, as was Franklin Roosevelt in the final months of his life, toward the conclusion of Word War II.

When supporting a leader who is ill we can bear in mind these guidelines:

> Our primary responsibility is to the common purpose and those whom the organization serves.

> We are also responsible for the welfare of the leader as a human being who is ill, and perhaps in pain and frightened.

> If the leader won't acknowledge the seriousness of her illness, we must help her do so or turn to whatever institutional recourse is available.

> Just as other courageous followers need our support from time to time, so may the leader's physician.

> If the leader will be unavailable for a period, we must clarify responsibilities and authorities so the organization can function.

> The leader needs reassurance that her interests and the interests of the organization are being taken care of so she can concentrate on recovery.

If we fail to temporarily reorganize in the face of a leader's illness, the organization can badly drift. If we regroup for the duration of the illness, we can make forward motion toward our purpose. When it's clear that the leader's team is in control of events, those who might otherwise take advantage of the leader's impairment will be dissuaded from doing so.

Illness tests leaders and followers. It is part of life. It must be acknowledged and dealt with both medically and organizationally. Faced with a leader's illness, the courageous follower takes energetic action to care for both the leader and the organization.

CONFLICT BETWEEN LEADERS

There is an African proverb: "When elephants fight it is the grass that suffers." When pursuing an organization's purpose, conflict will naturally occur. If managed well it can be productive. Conflict can also occur around ego issues, thinly masked in the guise of purpose. This is destructive conflict. When conflict occurs between two strong leaders who each have a large investment in the outcome of an issue—civic leaders, union presidents, heads of government—many people are at risk of getting trampled.

Turf war can take a great toll on a leader. While some appear to thrive on it, turf war absorbs creative energies and often leaves reputations and organizations wounded. The best chance of avoiding this destructive conflict, or ending it early, resides with the leaders' closest followers.

Warring leaders will apply emotional pressure for followers to support their positions. Loyalty may seem to demand that followers give in to the pressure, but the common purpose suffers if we do. Our higher responsibility is to help our leader find a course that serves the organization well. In doing so, our leader benefits, too. We can ask questions to put the issue into perspective:

What are the interests of each leader in this situation? What are the interests of the stakeholders?

Is continued conflict the best way of serving these interests or are there alternatives?

What are the risks in escalating the conflict?

What is the common ground between the leaders that can be built on?

Is there anything our side is doing to exacerbate the conflict?

What is the key thing each leader needs from the other to let go of the matter?

There are times, however, when asking these questions just of our own leader is insufficient. The acts of the rival leader (public accusations, false statements, deceitful maneuvers) may continue to throw our leader into extreme positions. It is a mistake in this situation to assume that the entire camp of the rival leader is supporting these inflammatory actions. In fact, we might assume that at least some of the rival's followers are trying to bring their leader back into balance.

Therefore, the power to de-escalate the conflict may well lie with us. It takes courage to suggest talking with "the enemy" when tempers are flaring. But the best approach may be to open a dialogue with the rival leader's followers about de-escalating the conflict. Working together, courageous followers from opposing camps may defuse their leaders' destructive conflict and avoid the damage caused by territorial feuds. In this way, each organization's purpose and leaders are well served.

FORMAL CHECKUPS

If leaders stumble, courageous followers help to pick them up and repair them. But we support a leader better when we practice preventive medicine.

It is wise to get a physical checkup periodically even though we feel healthy. We look in the mirror daily and know generally that we are well, but a formal medical checkup looks deeper, searching for incipient problems. It uses instruments to measure what our senses can't readily detect.

It is also wise for leaders to get checkups on how they are serving their organizations. Rarely are mechanisms in place for senior leaders to get performance reviews. Even lower-echelon leaders usually get reviewed by their superior, not by those they serve.

It takes courage for leaders to engage in a checkup process, as they don't know what it will uncover. Is there serious hidden disease? But just as the fear of cancer or heart disease warrants the periodic medical checkup, so should concern about the corrupting tendencies of power motivate the leadership checkup. When problems with power or relationships are caught early they are highly treatable; left to fester, they may prove deadly.

Various instruments for examination are available in the human resource department or through outside consulting firms. They measure a leader's own and others' perceptions of the leader's behavior. Followers should encourage leaders to use these instruments. Feedback distilled from a wide range of perspectives can serve as the equivalent of a CAT scan, examining many cross sections of leadership dynamics.

If the leader isn't accustomed to these types of checkups, the courageous follower makes a strong case for them. If the information gleaned is used sensitively and skillfully, it can save the leader and organization future grief, as does most preventive medicine.

There are many ways to support a leader. Courageous followers use the range of tools at their disposal. Our motivation in each case is our commitment to the common purpose and our regard for the leader.

4

THE COURAGE
TO CHALLENGE

FOLLOWERS WHO PROVIDE ROBUST SUPPORT for leaders are in a strong position to challenge them when their actions threaten the common purpose. Of the two broad areas in which we must be willing to challenge a leader—behavior and policies—the most difficult is behavior. It truly requires courage.

When I joined a struggling nonprofit organization, its entrepreneurial executive director had a plan to convert it into the marketing arm of a for-profit start-up. He had raised several hundred thousand dollars of venture capital and it seemed to him a good solution to the needs of both organizations. When he described the plan to me, I thought it was ill-advised.

The start-up would need a year or two to develop the software for its niche market and there was no guarantee it would succeed. Though the nonprofit was struggling, it had a history of being able to raise funds; it would no longer be able to do that if it gave up its tax-exempt status. This could kill the organization, which had a worthy purpose.

Though I was new to the organization, I was comfortable giving my feedback to the executive director, as there was nothing personal about it. The executive director accepted my feedback and put the plan on hold. It was a good thing, too, as the start-up folded in a couple of years and the nonprofit has resurged and is going strong ten years later.

On the other hand, when I worked in a large organization I encountered an influential and abusive division leader whom I didn't know how to stand up to, despite my years of service. She constantly disparaged members of other divisions, which divided and distracted the other divisions from the common purpose. She held a lot of political power in the organization and was personally very intimidating. Though I came from another division, I had her ear and might plausibly have given her the feedback she badly needed. But I couldn't bring myself to give her such sensitive, critical feedback about her personal behavior.

There are two unhappy outcomes to the story. One is that eventually I lost her ear and became one more victim of her venom toward "the other divisions." The other is that she continued to damage morale and, after involving the organization in illegal activity, was criminally indicted, dismissed from the organization, and served a prison term. If I had possessed the courage to challenge her, could I have changed this course of events? Only possibly, but I think that "possibly" makes trying worthwhile.

Devoted leaders and followers enter a kind of sacred contract to pursue their common purpose. They both are guardians of that purpose. Part of the courageous follower's role is to help the leader honor this contract. If we do not challenge a leader about dysfunctional behavior, the contract is slowly shredded before our eyes. The longer we wait, the less is left of the contract.

By not standing up to leaders, not only does the purpose suffer, so does our esteem for the leaders. This makes it harder to effectively give them feedback because it is difficult to do so when a relationship has deteriorated. The world may see a leader's attractive public persona but, as in marriage, those closest to the leader also see the less attractive patterns. If we do not air our concerns about behavior that threatens the common purpose, we begin to define leaders by these unattractive characteristics rather than by their talent and commitment. It is the responsibility of partners in a relationship to not let this happen.

In my corporate consulting I find it painfully common for staff not to tell their bosses what they need from them to do a good job: mundane things like holding fewer meetings and making them shorter, or giving fewer orders and letting people concentrate on getting the most important tasks done. Corporate leaders would be absolutely amazed at what they don't hear, because they'd find most of it inoffensive and worth considering. As followers, we need to start challenging our leaders on this level of process and policy when warranted. That will improve the organization's operation, strengthen the honesty of our relationship with the leader, and prepare us to deal with more difficult personal issues, should they arise.

Leaders with the strong egos and passionate vision needed to scale mountains are prone to self-deception. Some dynamic leaders are so invested in making their mark that they cannot let in information telling them it cannot be made in this way, at this time. A key role of a follower is to minimize this self-deception, to find ways of revealing reality to the leader. To stand up and remove the blinders from a leader's eyes is a daunting task when the leader is convinced he possesses x-ray vision.

In this chapter I present methods for getting through to leaders so they can hear what we have to say. I will discuss how to create an environment that supports creative challenge, that expects it rather than defends against it. The extreme importance of the courageous follower overcoming groupthink impulses is explored, as well as several serious dysfunctional behaviors that followers may encounter and need to deal with.

If we find the courage to stand up to our leaders, they may initially find it as uncomfortable as we do, but eventually they will see that we are also standing alongside them in their corner.

APPROPRIATE BEHAVIOR

Leaders occupy their positions because of some constellation of strengths. Many of these strengths are of great value to the organization. Other strengths may not be those the organization needs at this time, at least not in the intensity the leader is using them. For example, the organization may have benefited from great force of personality during its founding days and now requires more collaborative skills in its leaders. But if a leader believes certain behaviors were responsible for earlier successes, he will tend to rely on those behaviors in his current role.

Like all of us, leaders believe their actions are justified or they wouldn't take them. In the leader's case the evidence seems irrefutable—their leadership behavior got them where they are now! This conviction forms a barrier to self-examination. They don't notice that the current context differs from earlier contexts in which the approach was successful. Taking action that may have been appropriate at other places or times may be inappropriate now. Governor Clinton's hands-on management style may have served Arkansas well, but President Clinton needed to learn the limits of that style.

An incident in which old successful leadership behavior clashes with a changed environment can provide a courageous follower the opportunity to discuss these changes with a leader. The fallout from the incident may provide a ripe opportunity for helping the leader reexamine behavior. If events have piqued a leader's interest in the subject, a close aide might formally or informally guide the leader through this thought process:

In what situations has the leader been most successful?

What did the leader do in those situations that brought success?

What are the similarities between those situations and the current one?

What are the differences?

How important are the differences?

Has the leader been using any of the same strategies used in the earlier situations?

Are those strategies working as well as they previously did?

Given the different situations, what changes might improve the results?

This nonthreatening approach invites leaders to examine what is working and what isn't, what is appropriate and effective in the current environment and what isn't. We are not offering feedback, simply asking questions that help leaders analyze the results they are getting with their current leadership methods. Skillful questioning is the mildest form of challenge to inappropriate behavior, but it is potentially extremely effective.

PREPARING A LEADER FOR FEEDBACK

Feedback is the great mechanism of self-discovery. We take an action, watch its effects, and learn what works and what doesn't. When we are young this mechanism operates brilliantly.

As we develop and form our self-image, we start screening out feedback that contradicts that image. Preserving our internal sense of self becomes more important than learning and growth. We also may develop an external image we work to maintain. For those who become public figures—CEOs, principals, commanding officers, managing partners, politicians—protecting this public image may seem most important. More screens go up and the only messages that penetrate are the ones that validate our image of ourselves.

There is little value in standing up and giving leaders feedback they cannot hear. The courageous follower's role is to find ways leaders can receive the feedback they need. We can minimize defensiveness by prefacing our feedback with a defusing statement that conveys respect and reminds the leader of the value of honesty:

"You know how highly I think of your work and I hope you won't mind my speaking frankly."

"You know that I respect what you are trying to do and I'm sure you'd want me to be honest with you."

Leaders are more apt to pay attention to feedback if we link it to outcomes they desire, to what motivates them. Is it promotion? Profits? Reelection? Reputation? We certainly hope the list includes the common purpose. By linking our feedback about a behavior or policy to its impact on what leaders value, their interest in the subject outweighs the impulse to defend their image:

"I think what you are doing will affect _____ (what the leader values). May I give you my views?"

"I'd like to give you feedback on that. I think it's important to what you're trying to accomplish."

Another way to defuse defensiveness is to share our own struggles with the same or similar issues. We can point out similarities between our situations as well as differences. This creates empathy and may help the leader talk about the subject.

"I understand what you're up against as I had a similar experience with _____ ."

"I identify with your reaction because I have the same reaction when _____ ."

Giving a leader feedback about policies is usually easier than giving feedback about behavior, but not always. A leader may be completely wedded to a position that could have disastrous consequences. If a leader seems closed to hearing other viewpoints on an issue, we might approach the leader this way:

"I have several things to tell you that you may not want to hear, but this is why you need to hear them."

Then state the reasons why the leader should listen, including the potential consequences to his own interests and to the common purpose.

Only give feedback on policies when you have the leader's attention and he has a somewhat open mind.

Preparing a leader for feedback is the requisite to effectively giving that feedback.

GIVING A LEADER FEEDBACK

We need to give leaders feedback with the same care we prepare them for it. Poorly given feedback can be received as an attack rather than a caring act. The leader may strike back defensively, dissuading the follower from giving future feedback.

Negative feedback must be clearly directed at the specific behavior or policy, not at the leader himself. It is better for a follower to say, "When you never smile at people it makes them anxious" than to say, "You intimidate people." The leader can't change who he is, but he can change his behavior, smile occasionally, and help the people around him relax.

When giving feedback about behavior, we must clearly state:

what the specific behavior is;

what adverse effects it is causing;

how serious the potential consequences are should the behavior continue.

To reduce defensiveness, it is more effective to make statements relating how the person giving the feedback feels ("I" statements) than statements about what the person receiving the feedback is doing ("You" statements):

"My research shows that this policy will have several adverse consequences" rather than "Your policy will have adverse consequences."

"I feel strongly about honesty and think we should reveal the
information we have immediately" rather than "You're being dis-
honest by withholding the information."

The "I" statements are truer and more effective. They don't sound accus-
atory so are less likely to trigger defensiveness.

Of course, it's preferable to raise sensitive issues privately with leaders
just as we prefer them to do with us. This is difficult if a prominent leader
is always surrounded with aides. We may need to request a private audience or make a judgment call about giving feedback with others present.

It is important not to overdo feedback as we risk making the leader too
introspective. Leadership requires looking outward and forward. Some
people counsel making five positive statements for every criticism if we
want healthy relationships. Whether this exact number is necessary, the
principle seems sound. If someone gives us constant negative feedback, the
practice wears thin and we close ourselves off.

It is not appropriate or realistic to expect leaders to accept every piece
of feedback and immediately make changes. Feedback is not always on target. Sometimes the feedback is on target, but the timing is wrong.
Sometimes leaders need to stick to their positions. Leaders who change
their position every time they talk to someone else aren't leading.

Feedback is a critical and fragile element in the leader-follower system.
Leaders are fortunate to have followers who develop this skill and understand its appropriate use.

INVITING CREATIVE CHALLENGE

While feedback is a critical component of the leader-follower system, it is
reactive. Beyond feedback there is a proactive mode of operating in which
ideas are continuously encouraged, developed, examined, challenged,

modified, synthesized, and adopted or discarded.

A creative culture emerges when there is a commitment to broadening participation and seeking diverse perspectives, to challenging the status quo and the obvious solution. When a group relishes this spirit of creative challenge it rolls back its limits and finds new ways of pursuing its purpose.

An important role of the courageous follower is helping a leader distinguish between challenge to his authority and challenge to ideas. Viewing challenge as integral to continuous improvement permits an environment of open dialogue and vibrant creativity.

We need to understand how dynamic leaders inadvertently discourage creative challenge:

> **Leaders often grasp situations and opportunities with great internal speed and want to rapidly implement their ideas.**

> **Leaders are prone to communicating their ideas with great energy and conviction, which is part of their gift.**

> **A leader's premature display of conviction about an idea discourages creative challenge; a would-be challenger does not want to appear negative or disloyal.**

> **Leaders need to leave space for and invite creative thinking about issues or they deny the organization the full use of its resources.**

Too often, a CEO spends a whole meeting presenting a "great new idea" as a fait accompli, then asks if there are any problems with it. The people around the table know he's made up his mind and doesn't really want to hear about problems, so they don't speak up. There is no process that invites creative dialogue.

If a leader doesn't establish a norm of creative challenge, a courageous follower needs to energetically model and advocate it. This act can be more productive than any challenge we make to a specific position, behavior, or policy as it is central to a group being in healthy, creative relationship with each other and the leader.

The elements of a culture that embraces creative challenge include:

Information about situations of major import to the group is broadly shared.

Dialogue about important decisions that will impact the group is invited.

Sacred cows are gently led to pasture—all subjects are open for discussion.

To encourage uninhibited thinking, processes are established for generating creative approaches that are distinct from the processes for evaluating those approaches.

Distinctions are made between an idea and its originator so status does not cloud value; as appropriate, methods for anonymously presenting ideas are used.

Group members improve their communication and meeting skills so they don't discourage contributors through words, voice tone, or body language.

Even "wild" ideas are not discounted, but examined for new ways of thinking they may open.

Even "sensible" ideas are tested against different scenarios to see if they hold up under scrutiny.

Once leaders commit to a participatory creative process, followers can reinforce this commitment. Participation is essential when decisions are being made that have an impact on how the organization pursues its purpose and that rely on team buy-in to implement. If the leader falls back on old ways of decision making that preempt group input, the courageous follower challenges this:

"That's an extremely interesting idea—let's explore it at the staff meeting."

"You're raising an important point—let's get some other perspectives to make sure we're not looking at this too narrowly."

"That sounds promising but I'm disappointed you acted unilaterally when we've agreed that strategy changes will be reviewed at the senior management meeting."

"We've got a problem—if you keep acting outside the process we've established we can't give you the creative ideas you want."

It is up to followers to be clear about the value they place on consultation and participation. Leaders are politically shrewd. When their people feel strongly about something, they usually won't ignore it.

CHALLENGING INDIRECTLY

We can't always create an environment in which creative challenge is readily accepted. Sometimes a leader feels threatened by direct confrontation or doesn't value participatory processes. We may need to find ways that engage rather than alarm the leader when we want to challenge questionable ideas or behaviors. The problem is often the leader's fixation on one idea, solution, or viewpoint. These are the blinders that have undone leaders throughout history.

A courageous follower chooses the right tool to help a leader examine options and their potential consequences. It is important to expand our toolkit so that we have the ability to indirectly challenge ideas and behaviors if that elicits dialogue rather than defensiveness. Anything that gets the leader to step a little to the side in viewing something is helpful. It begins a questioning process that can reveal flaws in the plan, unearth ways of proofing it against failure, enhance its potential, or lead to better alternatives. Simple questions we may ask to shift perspective include:

"Is there another plausible interpretation of what has occurred?"

"Is there another way we can look at this situation?"

"Does anyone have a slightly different take on this?"

Another indirect approach is to pose questions that others might ask the leader about his policy or behavior. Rather than directly challenging the leader, we are preparing him for challenges others may make in the less supportive arena outside the inner circle. A follower should become adept at asking "questions we might expect" such as:

"How would we respond to the concern that _____ ?"

"Could that appear to conflict with our values on _____ ?"

"How might _____ interpret that?"

"How would we answer charges that _____ ?"

"What alternatives might our stakeholders want us to consider?"

"What would we say if asked about other options we considered and why they were discarded?"

Once a dialogue is opened, the leader's and followers' underlying concerns can surface, options can be explored, pros and cons weighed, possible outcomes tested. Even leaders who are open to creative challenge will find "questions we might expect" helpful in clarifying their positions.

AVOIDING KNEE-JERK REJECTION

Some people automatically reject new ideas or feedback. It doesn't matter what the idea is, it gets rebuffed. This is a version of the "not invented here" syndrome.

People who have been around awhile may be quick to say, "We've already tried that and it didn't work." It's not a considered rejection of the idea so much as a reflex. Even if they have already tried something, maybe times have changed or there's a different way to do it that will be successful. Being too quick to say "It won't work" shuts them off from exploring the idea and supporting continuous improvement.

A leader's "knee-jerk rejection" of ideas may just be a poor habit a follower can work around until the leader unlearns the habit. Like any habit, it takes time to shake. If we know a leader is prone to knee-jerk rejection we can try a "delayed response" tactic:

Briefly air our observations and recommendations with the leader.

Quickly, without engaging in extended dialogue, ask the leader "to think about it" so that the issue can be further discussed at a later point.

Even if the leader's automatic rejection mechanism triggers, ask the leader to "still think about it."

Don't ask for and don't accept an immediate response or decision.

We shouldn't be surprised if the leader raises the issue with us again and displays openness to our ideas once he has given them some thought. By getting out of his face, we let an internal dialogue occur that seems to shift the "win-lose" framework from which he originally viewed our suggestion or request. Reflection replaces reflex. And we can raise the issue again if the leader doesn't, often with success.

Followers who find themselves too quick to reject ideas or feedback can use the same tool. Instead of disagreeing we can say, "Let me think about that." If we really do think about it, we often find something in the idea we can use.

OVERCOMING GROUPTHINK

It is not only leaders who need to be challenged; sometimes a courageous follower must challenge the thinking of the whole group. Some groups are fractious and need help focusing on the common purpose. Other groups are cohesive; the members closely support each other, giving the group strength. Cohesiveness can become a weakness, however, if this close support develops into the need, almost regardless of cost, for unanimity. The value placed on concurrence supplants the central purpose of the group and becomes its primary, though unstated, agenda. Ideas that conflict with the group's policies and actions are, at best, offered weakly and withdrawn quickly if opposed. This phenomenon is known as "groupthink."

A symptom of groupthink is a group self-image of infallibility and superiority: "Whatever we do is excellent." Groupthink screens out data and views that challenge this image. It eases out people who offer conflicting views. It destroys creative challenge. The group becomes obsessed with its cleverness and importance, its power and image. It develops the illusion it is invulnerable to danger. Contemporary American history is strewn with examples of the consequences of groupthink, from Pearl Harbor to the Iran-Contra affair. The Clinton administration's health care initiative may well have suffered from groupthink. In contemporary corporate history, companies from General Motors to IBM have been furiously trying to break this mold.

Courageous followers should periodically encourage a group and its leader to question themselves:

> **Have we objectively compared ourselves with similar groups lately, or do we just believe we are superior?**
>
> **Are we using the right measures of success?**
>
> **Are our measures consistent with our values?**
>
> **Are we measuring ourselves or are we asking those we serve to evaluate us?**
>
> **Have we grown complacent about searching for new ways of accomplishing our purpose?**
>
> **Are other organizations doing innovative things that we should also consider?**
>
> **Have we become so sure of ourselves that we no longer critically evaluate even risky ideas?**

Are newcomers having to conform to our ways or are we also learning from them?

Are we failing to treat environmental changes seriously because we don't think they can affect us?

Groupthink causes self-censorship. We do not permit ourselves to acknowledge our own divergent thoughts. We relinquish responsibility for our unique perspectives, which is a terrible error. If other members of the group accept the organizational status quo, we invalidate our own discomfort with it, even if the status quo dramatically departs from our ideals.

To rise above groupthink we must trust ourselves. Trusting ourselves doesn't mean trusting that we are right, but trusting that we are relevant, that our perceptions are keen, that we have verified our facts, that our thoughts are meaningful and important. It is only the individual who can rise above groupthink and help the cohesive group and its leaders test their ideas and actions against reality. We need to pay attention to our "inner voice":

Am I uncomfortable with things others seem to accept?

Am I accepting things I would not accept in another environment?

Am I devaluing information that contradicts what is supposed to be happening?

Am I inhibited from acting on my perceptions because no one else seems to share them?

If we aren't confident enough to voice our feelings strongly, we can raise them tentatively and observe the responses we get. Do the responses satisfy or reinforce our concerns? If the group and leader dismiss our concerns out of hand, we should continue to be concerned. If they genuinely address our concerns, we are probably not dealing with groupthink.

THE DUTY TO OBEY

If we have courageously but unsuccessfully challenged a leader's policies, where do we stand in relation to implementing them?

The policies may be different from those we would have chosen; they may be fraught with risks with which we are uncomfortable; we may feel they have negligible chance of success. These are our views—they may or may not be right. The leader may be displaying brilliant prescience, which we do not share. Only time will reveal the outcome. What is our responsibility in this situation?

If we choose to continue being a follower of this leader and if the policies are not morally repugnant to us, we have the responsibility to implement the policies. It takes courage to follow leaders when we are not convinced they are right, courage to truly allow leaders to lead. It is our responsibility to give the policy a chance, to make it work through energetic and intelligent adaptation rather than allow it to fail through literal interpretation or lukewarm execution.

We have the right to challenge policies in the policy-making process; we do not have the right to sabotage them in the implementation phase. In the world of politics, we often hear of "leaks" intended to thwart a policy set by superiors or to forward the policies of a subgroup. Those who sabotage their leader's efforts are no longer followers; they are opponents.

Each of us has the right to become an opponent. But if we do so covertly, without declaring our opposition, while still holding our position and demeanor as a follower, we create havoc within the organization. We drive trust below a level where the group can remain cohesive. We create the opposite of a groupthink situation. We create factions and internal warfare that can threaten to immobilize or fracture the group and undermine the common purpose.

If we follow too slavishly we contribute to blind groupthink. If we can't follow at all we contribute to anarchy. If an organization is rife with leaks and acts of internal sabotage of the leader's policies, a courageous follower needs to look for the underlying reasons:

Is the policy-making process unfriendly to creative challenge, encouraging disaffected players to circumvent the process?

Is there lack of sufficient respect in the organizational culture for the policy-making process, and an inclination to nullify its outputs?

Are there one or more players who are truly not willing to follow and unwilling to support team decisions?

If the creative challenge process is so weak it breeds discontent, we may need to further challenge the leader to open it up. If it is already credible and open we may need to help the leader challenge individuals who are disregarding it or challenge the organizational culture itself to value it more.

Where serious disagreement exists, courageous followers may need to become courageous opponents. In all but the most repressive regimes, however, followers cannot become saboteurs and be called courageous.

THE DUTY TO DISOBEY

There are times when we cannot convince leaders to change their policies or actions and we gracefully line up with the team and support the policies. There are other times when the policies or actions are morally unacceptable to us. In this case a courageous follower must consider refusing to participate in their implementation.

The right to refuse and the duty to refuse implementing a policy or order are almost indistinguishable; they should be exercised under nearly identical circumstances. If we receive a policy or order that we feel is destructive to fundamental values and the common purpose, our right and duty to refuse to implement the policy or order activate. We have the duty to disobey even if the whole group obeys. This requires profound courage because the pressure to conform is enormous. Not only do we need the courage to voice our decision to disobey, we must also find additional courage to sustain our decision when we are cajoled or threatened into changing it.

In some circumstances we can formally query the policy or order, or appeal it to a higher level of authority, although sometimes the higher authority itself may be the root of the problem. In other circumstances there is no time for formality and we must make the decision on the spot. There are times when values conflict; for example, values formed in different cultures may be inherently polarized. Compassion, intelligence, self-esteem, and perhaps even a little higher guidance are needed to determine when refusing to comply is the correct and necessary action.

No fast rules can be devised to guide our decision to disobey; each act is one of principle taken within the context of a specific and unique situation. What kinds of circumstances might warrant refusing to implement a policy or order?

Human life or health are being unnecessarily risked.

Common decency is being violated.

The rule of law is being sacrificed to expediency.

The organization's purpose is being undermined.

The organization's stakeholders are being denied basic service.

A clique or special interest is being served at the expense of the common good.

It is even more important to reject a policy or order when others' rights and welfare are jeopardized rather than our own. This is how the fabric of the social order is kept whole. While disobedience on behalf of another may be more clearly defensible, the courage required is greater because there is so little to be gained for ourselves, so much to be lost.

When we take a courageous stance by refusing to implement instructions, we sincerely believe our actions are right and necessary. It may turn out, however, that our decision to disobey was wrong and carried serious consequences for the group. Fear of error should make us appropriately cautious, but not paralyze us. We have to be prepared to shoulder the responsibility for our mistakes, too.

The determination between insubordination and bravery is made in the formal and informal courts that review acts of disobedience. If courageous followers participate in these courts as judge or jury, they will carefully examine the motives that drove the acts. If the acts sprang from fundamental human values and decency, they will weigh that against the value of compliance to authority.

CHALLENGING ABUSE EARLY

In addition to challenging policies, we may have to challenge behavior that violates our values and undermines the common purpose. Corruption of values doesn't occur all at once. Usually, a series of small departures from an individual's values leads to larger departures. The nonprofit director's use of an organization's funds for personal items begins with petty expenditures and ends in grand larceny. If we fail to challenge small violations of values it becomes increasingly difficult to avoid the "slippery slope" of accelerating moral decline. When abuse of power becomes a way of life our chances of correcting this, or even surviving an attempt to correct it, greatly diminish.

When we have a very positive image of a leader, we may be too quick to rationalize behavior that doesn't conform to that image. If a leader proves strategically brilliant, we can get so enamored of this brilliance that we overlook small breeches of values. If we experience discomfort with a leader's actions, we must allow ourselves to experience it, not push the feelings away because they don't conform to our images.

It is essential to challenge abuse of power early:

> The *first time* the courageous follower encounters behavior antipathetic to the organization's values is the most important time to challenge the behavior, before it becomes a habit.

The challenge must be skillful and completely firm; an irresolute challenge will appear to sanction the behavior.

If the follower firmly and appropriately challenges the behavior, her courage and integrity will generate respect and the leader will be prone to listen to her in the future.

If the follower waits too long to challenge the leader's behavior, both the behavior and justification for it will harden and the follower may be viewed as a nuisance or threat.

When abuse is already entrenched, each new person who enters the leader-follower relationship has an opportunity to change the entrenched condition or be changed by it. The task is harder when abuse is entrenched, in some cases it may be dangerous, but a courageous follower can make a difference if she conveys concern and support in her challenge:

"As the new person here, I've been able to see things from an outsider's perspective. I think it's important you understand how things look from that perspective."

"I've observed practices that seem to have become accepted but will cause you trouble if not corrected."

"You brought me in to deal with problems you were having with the organization. In addressing them I've discovered deeper issues that may make you uncomfortable but are important for you to hear."

The road to integrity is paved with speaking up about and acting on small corruptions of principles as we encounter them; left unchecked, these moral potholes can become sinkholes that swallow the common purpose.

CHALLENGING THE USE OF LANGUAGE

Courageous followers are alert to the language of leaders as well as to their deeds. Language both shapes and reveals the beliefs underlying deeds. Pejorative words thrown about are predictive of the stones that may follow.

The use of derogatory terms to describe groups or individuals dehumanizes them and establishes the climate for abusive actions. The use of the words "yid," "nigger," "fag," or "slut" have all preceded lynchings, beatings, or rapes. Their public use is now considered outrageous, but their private use continues. Even mildly diminishing language creates an "us" and "them" mentality that justifies abuse.

It requires as much courage to confront a leader about language as about behavior; it is easy for the leader to ridicule our concern and claim the words were "unimportant" or "harmless." They are not. Confronting the leader about demeaning language is a critical opportunity for establishing a relationship of principled creative challenge. It is a variation of challenging abuse early.

When leaders use euphemisms (collateral damage, relocation centers, downsizing), we should challenge them to explore their underlying discomfort with a subject. Challenging a leader's use of language can flush value conflicts to the surface where they can be examined. Even syntax is deserving of challenge when it obscures responsibility for actions:

> "It's regrettable this happened" instead of "I'm sorry I did that."

> "Our policy has always been" instead of "I support the policy."

> "The budget didn't permit" instead of "We cut your request."

> "Civilians were killed in the bombing" instead of "We bombed and killed civilians."

We don't have to bludgeon leaders about their use of language. We can point out quietly what we just heard and our discomfort with it. Patterns of speech are so deeply ingrained that the leader may be unaware of how he used the words. We are providing the leader an opportunity to become aware of the language influencing his thoughts, masking his feelings, or coloring the messages he is sending.

History is papered over with language that obfuscates the abuse of power. By challenging leaders and groups to assume responsibility for their actions and the words they use to sanitize those actions, a courageous follower holds up a mirror that demands self-examination.

ARROGANCE

There are various attitudes and behaviors specific to individual leaders that, if present, need challenging. Arrogance is high on this list. Arrogant leadership is toxic to an organization. It looks like strength but is a debilitating weakness. If you have ever worked with an arrogant leader you know what a low level of tolerance and respect this type has for others. Arrogant leaders make the fundamental error of believing they are qualitatively different from their followers. Failing to perceive their commonality, they lack the spiritual requirement for a life of service. Instead, they build their careers on manipulation.

A courageous follower who is working closely with an arrogant leader must try to contain the effects of the leader's behavior, as difficult as this is to do. Arrogant leaders often denigrate supporters to each other, creating an environment in which no one knows where they stand and everyone is trying to curry favor. We may be tempted to collude with this denigration if it confirms our position as part of the inner circle. But we must realize that the denigration will soon be turned against the inner circle itself if it hasn't already.

We might attempt a containment strategy along these lines:

Get the leader's agreement that it would be good to build a stronger team; from his feeling of superiority, the leader will probably agree he needs a stronger team.

Get the leader's agreement that denigrating each other weakens the team.

Then exact a simple, but critical, commitment from the leader: that he will not demean team members to each other.

By curtailing demeaning comments, the whole atmosphere surrounding the leader can change. The fires of arrogance are not continuously being stoked.

Once we have an agreement, we can challenge the leader to honor it by expressing our discomfort with the denigration when it occurs:

"_____'s not here to clarify her actions so why don't we hold off discussing that."

"That may not hold up under closer scrutiny. Let me investigate and report back on that."

"I'm not comfortable impugning their intentions. Let's focus on what we need from them."

"We've agreed not to harp on our own people's shortcomings. What is our responsibility as senior management for the performance problems?"

This is an instance in which, by changing behavior, we can sometimes change the underlying attitudes. In the interest of the common purpose, it is worth trying.

LEADERS WHO SCREAM

Another behavior that must be challenged is chronic screaming by a leader. Explosive anger is intimidating and tears the fabric of relationships. Things get done, but at a very heavy price. The virtue in leaders who scream is their passion for the cause and their desire to shake up people who serve it complacently. Followers understand this. It is partly why they stay with strong leaders despite the extreme unpleasantness of the screaming behavior. Frequent angry outbursts, however, weaken both the self-esteem of followers and their bond with the leader. Abusive upbraiding is antithetical to the spirit of creative challenge. Innovative teams are not built of players who cower.

Followers are usually shocked and angry at the leader's abusive behavior. They do not realize that once a screaming pattern is established it is no longer under the leader's conscious control. The leader is often inwardly as dismayed by the outbursts as are the followers. It is true the leader is using anger to get his way, but he is not necessarily in control of the anger. Leaders may justify their rage in the name of the cause, but it is not justified. It is just out of control. For this reason injunctions against berating staff in front of others often fail.

Therefore, we should not allow new leaders to develop screaming patterns, but should challenge this behavior the first time it occurs. The norms preventing screaming loosen when one becomes the leader. The real and imagined pressures increase. This is a fertile mix for a screaming pattern to take hold unless it is immediately checked. If the leader is already established, but the follower is new to her position, she should follow the same rule and nip the behavior the first time it is directed at her.

The challenge for the follower is to maintain balance, to not freeze, and to not let the tantrum run unchecked. A follower can sometimes successfully impose limits on what is occurring until the leader regains self-control. The tendency, when confronted with a screaming authority figure, is to regress to the affect of a scolded child. It is critical to remain in an adult posture. Physical bearing, eye contact, tone of voice, and language can all help achieve this.

> "(John, Mr. Brown, Sir—whatever you usually call the leader), I want to discuss this. It's clearly very important to you. But I won't discuss it like this."

> If the leader can't calm down: "Let me give you a few minutes to collect yourself and I'll be back to address your concerns."

> Sometimes we need to risk screaming back at the leader, as this restores an adult balance to the relationship—though not an optimal one.

It is noteworthy that there are individuals with whom even renowned screamers will not display the behavior. If a follower challenges a leader firmly to treat her with respect, she may prevent an abusive pattern from taking hold in relation to herself. If the leader continues to scream at others, the courageous follower can use her own firm stand against screaming to help the leader contain his dysfunctional behavior. The follower who is not the immediate target of abuse is psychologically in a stronger position to respond.

If present when the leader explodes at a more junior person, a courageous follower can choose how to intervene. Some possibilities are:

> Make a firm statement and physically remove the abused person: "Excuse me. These are serious accusations. Let me establish the precise facts of what happened with _____ and get back to you in a few minutes. Please excuse us while we talk in the next room."

> Ask to speak with the leader privately, then and there. Once in private, confront the leader about the behavior: "You clearly have reason to be upset. But dealing with it this way is hurting you and the organization."

Intervening in these ways interrupts the destructive pattern and allows the leader to absorb the fact that the behavior is unacceptable in the eyes of third parties. In some cases, challenging the behavior will have a calming effect and the leader may stop displaying the behavior as frequently. In other cases, the leader may need additional help to regain control of and transform these excessive reactions, a case that we will examine in the next chapter.

Nearly everyone has worked at some time with a screamer. There are still plenty of screamers around but, like cigarette and cigar smoking, it is becoming much less acceptable. In addition, like the health risks of second-hand smoke, it is attracting the lawsuits one can expect in our litigious society. There are ways to get the job done that are healthier for everyone than screaming.

PERSONAL ISSUES

We may experience acute discomfort about challenging leaders when destructive behavior occurs in their personal lives. But distinctions between personal and public life are not very useful when behavior violates the values of the organization and the society in which the organization operates. It is our responsibility to challenge the leader's behavior if it threatens to undermine trust and the common purpose.

Personal issues are the most sensitive issues on which to challenge a leader. Financial irregularities, infidelities, sexual harassment, and substance abuse are all highly emotive. The leader's response may be sharp and to the effect that we are out of line. We must be prepared to stand our ground:

> "This is not something I would ordinarily raise, but I believe the organization's goals and your position are at risk if it is not addressed."

> "I know you would like to see this kept a private matter, but it is already being talked about widely and we need to talk about it, too."

> "I'm not any more comfortable about discussing this than you are, but everything we are working for is being jeopardized."

> "If this were to appear on the front page of the Times, you and our organization would be devastated. Let's discuss it before that happens."

We may feel outraged and betrayed by the leader's behavior, as we would if we discovered a family member doing something intensely destructive to himself or the family. When highly sensitive issues threaten to derail the leader and the organization, we need to convey how deeply we feel without attacking the leader and closing him off from our help.

NEWLY ELEVATED LEADERS

At different stages in their careers, leaders are prone to different behaviors that courageous followers may need to challenge. Leaders who are new to their positions naturally require special help from followers who have been with the organization longer and understand its nuances. Sometimes, however, a special phenomenon can occur that requires both support and challenge early on.

When leaders are suddenly elevated—promoted, appointed, or elected to senior positions—an abrupt change can take place. They are transported into another reality in which they believe they should act and be treated differently. As newly elevated leaders, they have no precedent for this experience and they grope in the recesses of their minds for models to guide their behavior. The model they access may be real, fragmentary, or even illusory. It may be their perception, accurate or not, of how other senior leaders conduct themselves—even leaders with whom they have worked and whose leadership styles they didn't like. In extreme cases, the model they access may be an image of how an historical figure behaved in an extraordinary situation that was extremely different from the new leader's current situation. But lacking a more reality-based model, they may unconsciously base their behavior on faulty or inappropriate models.

One newly elected member of the U.S. Congress, for example, was behaving abrasively to his staff. When challenged about this in a leadership development program, he became aware that he was acting like one of his party's giants who had been in Congress for several decades. Or at least, he was acting how he thought that national figure acted in his office.

Using inappropriate behavior models can create an unsettling atmosphere in which new leaders appear to suddenly change and begin acting very differently, often autocratically. They may become distant even from those who helped them achieve the new position. Power seems to have "gone to their head."

If this occurs, we need to engage the leader in dialogue as early as possible about who he is using as a role model:

> "Which leader do you admire? What do you admire about his leadership style? Do you find that style appropriate here?"

> "When you think about leadership, what do you envision? Does that seem consistent with the values you want this organization to have?"

> "How do you see your new role? What are you basing that on? Have you observed the reactions you're getting from others?"

While discussing the role model, the leader can examine the appropriateness and observe the consequences of his actions. Only then can the leader begin to fill the new role appropriately and serve the common purpose well.

LEADERS WHO HAVE OTHER AGENDAS

New leaders can bring other agendas to their position. Old leaders can develop new agendas while in their position. Other agendas are not in themselves bad; they may even be helpful. If other agendas motivate leaders to excel in their current work thus positioning them to achieve future goals, these other agendas indirectly serve the organization. If leaders are active in other organizations that bind them to the community, the organization may again benefit.

Sometimes other agendas don't help the organization, but they don't particularly hurt it either. Life is full of things to do and people are fascinating mosaics of interests and motivations. A leader excessively involved with other agendas, however, can serve an organization badly. For example:

Competing agendas can distract a leader from the organization's needs, such as when a CEO devotes excessive time to serving on other boards and making outside speeches.

A leader can misuse the organization's resources for personal projects with which he is absorbed, such as writing a book or running for political office.

A leader's preoccupation with an agenda, such as expanding his empire through acquisitions, can squander the resources an organization has, by diverting energy from its primary purpose.

If a leader's other agenda is hidden, such as a government official ingratiating himself with a company he would like to work for after retirement, the common purpose can be compromised.

Courageous followers who see leaders pursuing other agendas at the expense of the common purpose will challenge them as soon as their behavior becomes suspect. It may be that the leader is more motivated by the other agenda and should make preparations for a transfer of leadership so he can cleanly pursue the new purpose. Or it may be that the courageous challenge refocuses the leader on giving the common purpose the energy it requires.

CHALLENGE THYSELF, TOO

Creatively challenging another is a delicate act that must itself be uncorrupted. In relationships we are prone to find fault with the other before examining ourselves, and the leader-follower relationship is no exception.

Both the leader and follower who blame the other for disappointments must look inward to find their own points of responsibility. When these are identified, understood, and owned, we can more meaningfully help each other examine our respective roles.

Before challenging a leader, we might ask ourselves:

How objective am I being? Do I have my own ego-investment in this issue?

Is "the complaint" one that I've had with other leaders, and more probably a function of my own patterns than the leader's?

Have I had excessive expectations of the leader, which are now causing me to be excessively critical?

Is this truly an important issue, or one in which my own sensibilities may be exaggerated?

Do I have a personal agenda that I must disclose so that I do not break faith with the leader's trust in my counsel?

It is always more difficult to see ourselves clearly than to see others. If we feel on unsure ground, if we sense something familiar about our reaction, it may be wise to use someone else as a sounding board before we challenge the leader. Courage in relationships starts with an honest examination of ourselves.

5

THE COURAGE
TO PARTICIPATE IN
TRANSFORMATION

 I FIND IT TRAGIC that able leaders who fall dramatically from grace often share a common experience: their closest followers have long been aware of their fatal flaw and were unsuccessful in getting the leader to deal with it. Revelation of the flaw often comes as an unexpected shock to the broader group because it has been carefully managed and kept from public view. But those closest to the leader have usually spent long hours dealing with the fallout from the leader's behavior and discussing among themselves what to do about it.

When a political leader self-destructs it is front page news, so we are more aware of this problem in the political world than in the business world. Presidential candidate Gary Hart's dare-the-press-to-find-out wom-anizing ended his plausible aspirations for the Democratic nomination. Former civil rights activist and Washington, D.C. mayor Marion Barry's cocaine habit and late-night hotel rendezvousing ended in a sting opera-tion and jail sentence. Senator John Tower's public inebriation cost him the otherwise certain confirmation as Secretary of Defense. President Nixon's paranoia led him to encourage and cover up the dirty tricks that eventually forced his resignation. Former New Hampshire Governor John Sununu, President George Bush's tough chief of staff and a classic example of some-one simultaneously serving as a follower and a leader, was driven out of office for his arrogant behavior.

What a terrible waste it is to lose a leader's talents because of one undesir-able behavior. In nearly every case there were undoubtedly a few who tried to confront these leaders about their behavior and were either ignored, refut-ed, given unkept promises, or shunted out of the inner circle. But the fact that they tried tells us that the courage to challenge isn't always sufficient.

Behavior that flagrantly violates values may be symptomatic of a deeply ingrained psychological pattern or an addiction, which takes more than a request to change. We can't tell leaders something once and then abandon our accountability for the impact of their behavior on our common pur-pose. Challenging something once does not give us the right to lean back cynically and say, "Well, they never listen!" We must search for approaches that reach our leaders and methods to help them transform the damaging behavior.

This requires courage for several reasons. First, we have to admit to ourselves how serious the situation actually is, how gravely it endangers the organization's work. Second, we may have to examine our own collusion with the leader's behavior, what we do that allows it to continue. Third, transformation is an inexact activity and can easily fail, leaving us the discredited champions of a very lost cause.

Some people don't believe transformation is even possible. Our culture tells us "You can't teach an old dog new tricks." I had one foundation reject a proposal I had written to fund an ethics workshop for members of the U.S. Congress and their staffs because "the individual's moral character is formed by early adulthood and can't thereafter be changed." This same skepticism is at work in the debate in the United States on crime—is there value in prevention and rehabilitation programs or should we just lock the criminals up?

The attitude that people can't change is defeatist, and I want to vigorously challenge our thinking on this subject in relation to leaders and followers. I can't responsibly write about challenging and leaving leaders without also writing about transforming. That option must be explored. It's easy to write someone off. It's also lazy and wasteful to do so if it can be avoided.

I believe that one of the most important advances of the closing decades of the millennium is the increasing use of transformative techniques, as imperfect as they may be. This may turn out to be the lasting contribution of the controversial "sixties" generation. For example, we see widespread acceptance of "twelve-step" programs for a wide range of addictions. We have become compassionate and sophisticated about helping war veterans and disaster victims process their trauma. Marriage counseling and family therapy are more frequently used today as options to slow the alarming divorce rate generated by the sexual and social revolution of the sixties and seventies.

At the same time that we see an increased use of transformation techniques, we see many failures in transformation attempts: the family member who keeps reverting to drugs, the war veteran who commits suicide, the marriage that fails despite counseling. Even more disturbing are the things about ourselves we would like to change, but have never been successful at changing. These make it hard for us to believe in transformation.

It is true that transformation is extremely difficult, often the most difficult challenge of our lives. I believe that we must, nevertheless, open up to its possibilities. If a behavior threatens to overwhelm our larger purpose, we must find the skilled help to support a transformation effort, muster the courage to go for it, and exert the discipline required to achieve transformation.

Transformation efforts should be attempted when a practice or behavior that violates the organization's values and threatens its purpose is so entrenched that it is barely understood to be a legitimate problem, let alone one of potentially catastrophic dimensions. When the practice or behavior begins to eclipse the positive contribution the leader is making to the organization, or the organization is making to its stakeholders, and the root of these behaviors is deeper than can be reached through everyday interaction, transformation is needed.

The transformation can be goal-oriented or process-oriented—for example, to clean up the impact the organization's practices are having on the environment or to improve the way its leaders involve others in decision making. Often, it can be both.

Sometimes the need for transformation arises out of external challenges that demand deep cultural change in the organization. But the change can only occur if the organization's leaders examine their values and beliefs, and practice dramatically different behaviors. This has been the experience of a host of Fortune 500 companies in the face of fierce international competition. A whole consulting industry has grown up around the need to help leaders and their organizations make fundamental changes in their ways of doing things.

Sometimes the need for transformation is precipitated more narrowly by personal behavior that threatens to discredit the leader and, by association, the organization. William Aramony, the dynamic head of the United Way who ceased to respect the boundaries between the organization's funds and his own, is a classic example. When the scandal became public he was removed in disgrace as head of the charitable organization he had developed into a national force, but many of the local chapters continued to see their contributions hurt by the breech of trust. There is far less support available for dealing with a leader's personal need for transformation, and there are far fewer obvious sources of help for these sticky situations, than for dealing with organizational change.

There are often strong internal and external pressures working against a leader's transformation. I have personally experienced some of these pressures. At one time I had a deserved reputation for being a screamer who used threatening behavior to get things done. I didn't like my out-of-control anger; it obviously hurt people and depressed morale. But I used my track record of turning around poorly performing offices to justify it. The behavior served me well in a high-pressured, results-now environment. Though I was ashamed of how out-of-control the behavior was, I was defensive when anyone intimated it was wrong.

Eventually, the behavior caused enough serious problems in my professional and personal life, and enough discordance with my basic value system, that I achieved some success in modifying it. But when organizational performance lagged, headquarters questioned whether I was going soft! It was only after leaving this culture and joining a different organization, which wouldn't tolerate abusive behavior and presented me with other models of success, that I was able to truly transform it in my professional life.

Sometimes the need for personal transformation and organizational transformation are intertwined. An organization may desperately need to move from a centralized command-and-control culture to a decentralized, risk-taking, service-oriented environment. But the organization can't effectively make this change until its leaders deal with their own exaggerated control needs. Transformation needs to be stimulated in both dimensions.

Too often, leaders do not become sufficiently motivated to engage in the tough job of changing their behavior until they have lived through a crisis precipitated by the behavior. By then the damage is usually extensive. Some people believe the motivation for transformation can't be developed short of a crisis. It is my view that the role of courageous followers is to preempt that crisis by engaging the leader in transformation before the storm.

When dealing with a hard-bitten leader, the prospect of transformation may seem hopeless; the leader may seem unapproachable on the subject and our efforts may cause a backlash and worsen the situation. But there are times when transformation must be attempted by a courageous follower, despite the risks. When we have a purpose we believe in and a strong, committed leader, it is worth all the effort to transform potentially tragic flaws.

Ask hard-bitten leaders who have been derailed by their flaws if, in retro-spect, they don't wish their followers had tried harder to get through to them.

This chapter focuses primarily on helping a leader with the process of personal transformation. It is based on my own observations and reflec-tions, on my personal transformation efforts, and on the few studies that have been done by others attempting to help senior executives change. I hope to provide some useful guidance, and don't pretend to present a definitive approach to transformation for leaders or followers. Extensive dialogue and investigation is needed on this subject. I begin this chapter with a statement of general principles, which the literature on human change suggests are true in any transformation effort. I also examine how resistance to change, which is present in all transformation efforts, mani-fests in particular in leaders. And most germanely, I explore what a coura-geous follower's role should be in a transformation effort.

It is very challenging for both leaders and followers to do the internal work necessary for transformation while keeping things going externally in their professional and personal lives. In the following pages, explore with me how the process might work.

WHEN IS TRANSFORMATION POSSIBLE?

Consciousness of the need for transformation can occur when leaders have gradually prepared for change and are ready to embrace it, or when they are unprepared for it and life events force them to wake up.

Usually, multiple life events contribute to an individual's or group's readiness for transformation. For example, a leader may be aware that her industry is going through profound changes, the exact shape of which won't be clear for years. At the same time, she may have attended a conference at which she heard another leader describe experiences preparing an organization to deal with these changes. And she may have had a taste of the power of transformative interventions at a leadership development program she attended. The combination of these events sparked commitment to change, to exploring new visions of what she and the organization could become.

Often, the combination of events that opens a leader to change, especially of a personal nature, is less positive. The organization has lost significant revenues. There have been disaffections from its senior ranks in reaction to the leader's authoritarian style. Negative press stories are further hurting morale. The stress of handling the job is having painful ramifications on the leader's personal relations. Perhaps she has developed serious physical symptoms from the stress. Too often, failure or trauma—divorce, heart attack, scandal, loss of position, prosecution—occurs before a leader opens to transformation.

The essential steps that make transformation possible are the acknowledgment of the need for change, the admission of blemish, the owning of some responsibility for the current state of affairs, and a glimpse of the potential to become something better.

THE PROCESS OF PERSONAL TRANSFORMATION

Let's examine what the process of transforming attitudes and behavior consists of, as well as the forces that can impede or facilitate the process.

SELF-ORGANIZING PROCESSES

Though many living things transform themselves, we don't expect a caterpillar to become an eagle, a tadpole to become a fox, or an acorn to become an apple tree. Every life form has its own mature potential. Similarly, we cannot expect an individual to radically change her personality, but we can expect and encourage that individual to evolve to her full potential.

Each human being has a core personality. That personality is formed and held in place, at least in part, by certain "core ordering" processes. These include how we organize experience into our view of reality, how we form our sense of identity, how we rank our values, and how we try to control our environment. Because these processes form the core of "who we are," they are very durable and not easily subject to change. They make us recognizable to our college classmates at our twentieth reunion, and to ourselves as we pass through the stages of our lives. But they are not immutable.

DISCOMFORT, THREAT, AND CRISIS

Human beings generally maintain a dynamic state of balance until faced with a dramatically new situation in the form of a novel opportunity, a unique challenge, or a crisis. Then we either accommodate to these events and achieve a new dynamic balance, or our framework for life begins to unravel.

When we experience too much threat to our core ordering processes we try even harder to use our old solutions. If these fail, we may experience a "breakdown"—physical, emotional, mental. The pain of the breakdown serves the function of demanding that we pay attention to our need to change.

RESISTANCE

It is completely usual to resist change even when we see change is desirable or necessary. We are fearful that we will lose important parts of ourselves that have made our lives work up to now. We can respect this resistance and its self-protecting purpose without succumbing to it. We can allow it to modulate the pace of change to a rate we can tolerate, without letting it sentence us to stagnation. We will find ourselves alternately opening and closing to the prospect of change. If we honor these natural fluctuations, we can use them to enter and retreat from new territory until we have surveyed it, chosen our preferred positions, and incorporated them into our core processes.

DEVELOPING UNDERSTANDING

As we open to the need for change, we observe more about our relationship to ourselves and our relationships to others. We observe how we feel and what we do in a particular situation; and we observe the consequences of these feelings and actions.

Observation is the first step in reengineering a process. We need to know exactly what the current process is and exactly what needs it serves. Then we can consider how to change it, how to get legitimate needs met more efficiently and thoroughly. We must understand our current patterns, their depth and force, and how much we rely on them. Then we can do the hard work of transforming them.

WILLINGNESS TO EXPERIMENT

As we open to transformation, we realize that the way we have done things, which seemed to be the only way things could or should be done, is not in fact the only way. And it may not be the best way. We begin to explore the options open to us.

We may try doing the opposite of our ingrained response, testing what it feels like to use nonhabitual behavior. We may let our recessive traits come to the fore and see what effect they have. It can be a small behavior we do differently, like listening at a meeting rather than jumping in early with forcefully made arguments.

Usually, the sustainable options open to us are not those at the other end of the spectrum. They may be a few degrees further in the direction we would like to go. We may place a little more value on something we previously ignored and a little less value on something we previously held sacrosanct—for example, a little less value on a deadline and a little more value on the impact of the deadline on ourselves and our family. We experiment and evaluate the results.

INTEGRATION

We cannot form a clear vision of realistic and desirable outcomes before we begin a transformation process. Transformation takes us from the known to the unknown. As the process unfolds we begin to envision new, desirable states. Often they are more complex than we could articulate at the outset, involving the integration of different factors—the hard and soft, the dark and light sides of our personality. When we can visualize a realistic outcome we can use it to guide and measure our progress. We can refocus from what was "wrong" to what we are becoming

The process of personal transformation moves from disorienting, threatening beginnings, to sobering and eye-opening middles, to invigorating and rejuvenating outcomes. It requires courage to stay with this volatile process.

THE FOLLOWER'S ROLE

In all situations calling for transformation, the people closest to the individual in need of change play a pivotal role. Our primary relationships are the arena in which transformation of attitude and behavior is most likely to occur. As followers who are close to a leader, we have the power to play that pivotal role:

> We can complicitly deny the need for transformation and cover it up, or we can openly contrast existing behaviors against desirable behaviors.

> We can tolerate abusive or dysfunctional behavior, or we can draw a line in the sand.

> We can fall in step with disruptive behavior, or we can model functional ways of interacting.

> We can judge and rail against leaders' failings, or we can see some of their struggles in ourselves.

We can create a hostile environment in which leaders fight for their lives, or we can provide the support they need to experiment and learn about personal change.

The paradox of transformation, from the follower's perspective, is that it cannot be achieved by focusing solely on the leader. Such a focus can become obsessive and manipulative. If we wish to help a leader transform, we must ourselves be willing to participate in the process of transformation. We need to examine our own role in the relationship with the leader. That is the only role we potentially have full power to change. We need to notice what *we* do that enables and colludes with a leader's dysfunctional behavior. For example, do we cower each time the leader throws a tantrum, and then frantically execute her barked orders? This reinforces the leader's experience that tantrums are the way to control the environment. If we change that part of ourselves, the leader may make adjustments to find a new fit with us.

While the balance of the chapter will discuss how a courageous follower supports a leader's transformation efforts, followers may want to seek similar support for their own transformation efforts.

THE FOLLOWER AS CATALYST

The task of courageous followers who see life's harsh wake-up call coming is to effectively make a leader aware of the need to preempt that call. This is often much harder than it sounds. Anyone engaging in dysfunctional behavior has a lot of defenses built up around it and a lot of filters in place to screen out messages that disconfirm their behavior.

How do we get leaders' own alarm bells ringing? How do we provide a simulator in which they can experience potential disaster without actually going through the crash that will damage both themselves and, very likely, those they should be serving? Courageous followers can become both amplifiers and interpreters of the events they want a leader to pay attention to.

Though leaders are probably aware, to some degree, of their problematic behavior, motivation to transform is only created when they realize how seriously others view it. This is a central point for courageous followers to comprehend:

> Because offending leaders rationalize the seriousness of their actions, they assume others will also minimize that seriousness. This is their fatal error in judgment.

> Conveying the intensity of our dismay, our concern, our outrage about the leader's practices is the single most important act courageous followers can take as catalysts for change.

If we understate our feelings out of deference to a leader's position, out of discomfort with vocalizing the truth as we see it, or out of fear of the leader's reaction, we will be ineffective as agents of change. The skill required is to deliver the message in a way that conveys our support for the leader without pulling punches. We can do this if we target the behavior, not the leader:

> "You and I share a deep commitment to the purposes of this organization. We cannot let those purposes be jeopardized by denying the serious impact _____ [dysfunctional behavior] is having on the organization."

> "Once you grasp the importance of an issue, no one is more capable of vigorously addressing it than you. I am very afraid that _____ [dysfunctional behavior] is bringing this organization to the brink of disaster."

> "If I were doing something that jeopardized my career, I know you wouldn't quietly let me drive over the cliff, and I can't let you do that either."

> "You've led this organization brilliantly, but we can't let that obscure how these actions are violating common decency."

Transformation occurs most readily in an atmosphere of "tough love"— a genuine appreciation for the person and a steadfast stance against the behaviors that are detrimental to the person and the organization. We each have our issues and time for transformation, and in healthy relationships, we take turns being a clear-eyed and resolute catalyst for the other.

CHANNELING
THE LEADER'S FRUSTRATION

Some leaders in need of serious self-examination experience frustration with the failings of others and do not make the link to failings in themselves. Rather than this presenting a problem, it may present an opportunity to involve the leader in a transformation process.

Especially if a leader explodes or dissolves under criticism, it may be more effective to first mirror back to the leader the difficulties she is reporting with others before confronting her with her contribution to the situation. Mirroring consists of paraphrasing the leader's frustration and communicating it back to her in a way that shows she has been heard, empathizes with her feelings, and reflects her self-image so she feels understood and appreciated. For example:

> **"I see that you are trying to weld together a first-class team that provides the best service possible. It must be extremely frustrating that not all of your people seem to be getting the idea."**

Once the leader feels understood, the follower can suggest a thorough review of the organization's systems to get at the root problems. Reviewing systems rarely seems threatening. A leader who is frustrated with a staff's performance is often open to such a suggestion, genuinely thinking the problems are "there," not "here."

From a systems perspective, great leadership and great followership are part of the same system. Though leaders may not be able to meaningfully hear that a system review will include examining their own role in the system, they need to be briefed on this for both ethical and practical reasons. Leaders' acceptance that they *may* be involved in performance issues opens the door to a review of their style and impact. If the leader is, indeed, a primary cause of system dysfunction, this will emerge in the review. Followers, of course, must be prepared to discover their own contribution to the dysfunctional system.

Whoever conducts the review will need to confront both the leader and followers about their roles in the dysfunction. The same caveat applies as was given to the follower-as-catalyst: to generate the motivation to change, the confrontation must clearly communicate the intensity of feelings within the group about the behavior and practices discovered in the review.

DENIAL AND JUSTIFICATION OF BEHAVIOR

The greatest barrier to changing dysfunctional behavior is denial or justification of the behavior. Leaders are prone to discount the importance of their destructive behavior on the grounds that up to now it hasn't prevented them from attaining success.

Often, however, the leader has been successful because of a less extreme and more functional version of this behavior, or because of another trait used in tandem with the destructive behavior. Vices and virtues are extensions of the same underlying quality. If courageous followers can help a leader distinguish between the destructive behavior and a related virtue, and can affirm the importance of the virtue, they may be able to open the leader to transformation:

> "You've always inspired people with graphic visions of a better future and made a positive difference in their lives. What you're doing now is different because it's covering up information and misrepresenting this investment as more attractive than it is."

"You may think it's the staff's fear of your anger that gets them to do what you want, but it's actually your determination and commitment. The anger just erodes their willingness to support you and the organization."

"Hubris" is that marvelous classical word that sums up the danger to those who have experienced success. It is defined as "insolence or arrogance resulting from excessive pride." It can be lethal to the leader and the common purpose.

History and the daily newspaper are strewn with examples of hubris brought to its knees, of successful lives ruined by self-defeating behavior: billionaires sent to jail, CEOs ousted by boardroom rebellions, national figures tarred by prejudices that slip out in public speech, labor leaders pilloried for misappropriating funds, celebrities dead from drug overdoses. We may need to remind the leader of such stories in painful detail. Each form of hubris has its examples, its warnings for others. The individuals in these examples were also once in exalted positions, too successful to heed warnings up until the moment of their downfall.

If ever courage is called for, it is when followers need to confront supremely confident leaders who are at the pinnacle of their careers, and tell them that their hundred-foot yachts are about to run into reefs and sink unless they make a radical change in course. If successful leaders are fortunate, they will have courageous followers in their crew.

DEDICATION TO CAUSE AS JUSTIFICATION

Leaders sometimes use their dedication to the cause to justify inappropriate behavior, and then construe a challenge to their behavior as an attack on the cause. Leaders may come to consider their own welfare so critical to the success of the organization that they justify anything they do for themselves, regardless of its appropriateness, on the grounds that it enables them to better serve the organization. Financial improprieties and misuse of the organization's resources are particularly prone to this type of justification.

Failure to maintain the boundary between the self and the organization or cause is one of the most dangerous confusions of identity a leader can experience. This is especially true when the leader is the founder of the organization, and the group itself confuses the identities of the leader and the organization. A courageous follower can approach this situation in several ways:

> At a functional level, we must try to help the leader see the consequences of her behavior and how it is hurting the very cause that represents her life's work.

> At a deeper level, we can try to help the leader identify her underlying needs and find ways of satisfying these that are more appropriate than her existing behavior.

> At the most profound level, we may need to encourage the leader to reclaim her own identity and separate it from the organization or cause.

There are times when a leader's identity is so completely immersed in the organization or cause that transformation is not possible; you cannot change something that you cannot find. In this situation, the leader must reclaim some of her independent identity as a prerequisite to change. A radical shift of environment, activity, power relationships, and focus, even for just a month, may create the fresh perspective needed. Opportunities for a leader to take a break that will help reestablish her boundaries with the organization include:

> a senior executive development program at a prestigious school or one of the better, transformationally oriented management institutions;

> an extended family vacation, far from the seat of her power, at the urging of family and friends;

an appointment to a demanding public-service position that engages the leader differently for a period;

a sabbatical to write, research, or rejuvenate;

a spiritual retreat at a center maintained for these purposes by the leader's religious denomination, or at one of a growing number of nondenominational spiritual retreat facilities;

a residential rehabilitation facility if substance dependency has entered the picture.

Sometimes senior executives arrange these breaks for themselves by having heart attacks or other life-threatening problems that motivate them to review their values and open themselves to transformation. Courageous followers provide gentler alternatives for leaders to step back and reclaim important parts of themselves.

REACTIONS TO CONFRONTATION

The act of inviting a leader to join in a transformation process itself initiates change. Raising an issue with a leader ensures things will never be quite the same, even if the change produced is subtle, and whether or not the change is positive from your perspective. We really do live in the universe described by quantum physics, in which even the act of bearing witness to an event changes that event.

When we invite leaders to join in a transformation process, we are probably going to generate some confusion and discomfort. They may wonder:

What exactly are these people asking of me?

Don't they think well of me?

What are their motives?

Is there danger in this?

How far am I willing to go with it?

Is this really necessary?

We must be willing to make the leader uncomfortable when we challenge her behavior. She may experience anger at being confronted, or depression because her positive self-image is being called into question. These are often necessary stages before acceptance can occur. We must be willing to deal with the leader's reaction, and the discomfort that may cause us, if we are to form an effective transformative relationship.

For transformation to occur, relationship rules need to change. We cannot relate at a superficial level. We need to be open and take risks. We can't ask a leader to transform dysfunctional behavior and hide it at the same time. When we invite a leader into a transformative process, we must be prepared to see what's under the visible part of the iceberg, to experience that too. We need to do this as compassionate adults who have power and choice in the relationship, who are asking to see the whole person, not as children who only want to see our parents' nurturing side.

If leaders vehemently disagree with our assessments, it doesn't mean we have failed. We may have started a process in which the leader asks, "Why am I getting these reactions from people?" Confronting leaders does not mean insisting that they see what we see about them. We may perceive part of the picture, or perceive it with partial accuracy. Others will perceive different parts, as in the parable of the blind men who each describe only the part of the elephant they can feel.

We can't let a leader off the hook about what we perceive. We may need to press our point hard. But only until the leader starts to get the message that something about her behavior is amiss and needs attention. At that point we must respect the leader's ability to identify the parts of the problem that her core ordering processes will allow her to begin addressing.

Raising consciousness means getting leaders to see what *they* can see, to expand their perception so they see more than they do now, so they get a sense of their blind spots. We can tell leaders what we see, but this is just a

starting point to get their attention. The task is to get them looking in a
direction they would rather not look, to awaken their interest in doing so,
to get their own considerable energy involved in the process.

IDENTIFYING
TRANSFORMATION RESOURCES

Once we have the attention of a leader and have interested her in transforming her behavior or practices, we should be prepared to suggest vehicles for doing so. While some of the process of transformation can be done
on our own, most people find it requires support from others or professional guidance. We will probably encourage a planned intervention, a selected
set of actions that will help the leader and group move toward desired outcomes. The approach we recommend will grow out of the conditions we
are trying to address:

> If the issue involves group dynamics, such as a nonparticipatory,
> autocratic decision-making style, an intervention is needed that
> addresses team processes.

> If the issue is personal, such as substance abuse, then individual
> counseling, rehabilitation, and a support group are indicated.

> If the issue concerns abuse of power, such as the questionable use
> of funds, an intervention will need to establish external controls
> as well as address internal psychological issues.

> Often a combination of interventions is needed to clarify values
> and vision, improve team skills and processes, and examine what
> underlies individual attitudes and behaviors affecting those
> processes.

> Sometimes it is best for the leader and followers to go through a
> transformational intervention together.

At other times it is preferable for the leader to participate in an experiential learning process with peers from other groups.

In some cases working with real issues is preferable, while in others it is more productive to use simulations and group exercises.

Whatever permits participants to experience and name the current state, to understand the price it exacts, and to name and desire a preferred state to work toward can be a transformative vehicle.

Consulting with professionals as needed, courageous followers examine the range of intervention choices and select appropriate modalities to recommend. We have to weigh the pros and cons of different approaches. For example, if we are considering recommending professional counseling as an option, the advantages include its potential for getting to issues below the surface as well as the fact that it is privileged communication. A disadvantage may be that the confidential nature of the process makes it hard for followers to know what's happening and inappropriate to inquire.

Whatever approach is suggested, it is often helpful for the leader and other participants in the process to have a clearly assigned partner, coach, or mentor—someone who is available to provide support between formal interventions. For the leader this might be a board member, a senior member of the staff who is respected for good judgment and fairness, or a former executive of the organization. Coaches can observe the progress of the transformation process, provide a reality check on our perceptions of change, and be advocates for the leader or ourselves as we each struggle honestly, but not always successfully, to make desired changes.

USING AN OUTSIDE FACILITATOR

If a group intervention is indicated, it is advisable to use an outside facilitator unbiased by preconceptions and uninvolved with organizational politics. An outside facilitator can ask difficult questions, make difficult observations, and be trusted to respect the confidentiality of the process. Otherwise our tough job is made even tougher. We are part of the change process. It's hard to both facilitate it and be part of it. They are different roles.

Retaining outside professional help is usually understood by the leader and accepted as a sensible approach. Occasionally a leader may object to the suggestion, saying, "What am I paying you for if we need someone else to fix this?" This is a curve ball. Organizations retain specialists all the time for special assignments: a legal department retains outside counsel, a marketing department hires advertising agencies, a personnel department uses executive search firms. Courageous followers make this case forcefully if the situation warrants outside support.

If a leader is uncomfortable with the prospect of a formal intervention, followers can help the leader overcome the discomfort:

> **Discuss the safeguards established in the process to protect the leader's self-esteem, public image, and sensibilities.**
>
> **Find peers who have been through similar processes and encourage the leader to listen to their experiences.**
>
> **Discuss the range of possible interventions and find one with which the leader feels comfortable.**
>
> **Arrange for the leader to meet with potential facilitators of these interventions to develop familiarity and trust.**

The more leaders understand and buy into the process, the greater the chance they will be fully engaged as it unfolds. As change agents, it is the responsibility of both the follower and the facilitator to help participants, including the leader, understand and open up to the process.

Sadly, there is still somewhat of a cultural taboo against personal counseling, which may be part of the optimum intervention. Particularly in public life, some people see a leader's need for therapy or counseling as calling the leader's fitness for office into question. This attitude is a terrible disservice to our leaders and ourselves. It denies our leaders tremendous growth opportunity and it denies us the benefit of self-examined leadership. This attitude is changing, however, among public figures, including the current president and vice-president of the United States. They understand the value of exploring and repairing old personal or family issues that may interfere with their optimal performance.

If a leader does seek professional counseling to address the underlying causes of intractable behavior, it should be construed as a sign of strength, not weakness, and should be fully supported and defended by courageous followers.

CREATING
A SUPPORTIVE ENVIRONMENT

Transformation requires a secure vessel—the equivalent of a protective cocoon in which the work can be done. This is difficult to create in the hurly-burly world of fast-moving organizations. It can be done, however, by followers who are committed to creating a caring community.

We sometimes hear of the loneliness at the top of an organization. Leaders do often feel alone, though sometimes the aloneness is of their own making. We need to communicate that they are not alone in their transformation efforts. We will support them and stand by them. We will share responsibility for the progress of the transformation effort with them.

Sooner or later, whatever the method used to become aware of existing behavior patterns and their impact, the leader needs to experiment with changing these patterns. Experimentation requires a supportive environment. Trying different ways of doing things will initially feel awkward or unnatural. We don't know what is going to happen when we experiment. It's okay to fall off the bike when we're learning to ride, as long as we won't get laughed at. Or run over. Experiments produce both excitement and anxiety.

How do courageous followers create a supportive environment in which leaders can move through a transformation process? Here are some guidelines:

Let leaders know we see their willingness to take on the challenge of transformation as a sign of their strength as a leader.

Continue to communicate clearly about the impact of their behavior; sustain the external pressure that requires them to generate enough internal pressure to avoid deflation of the transformation effort.

Show patience: remember the strength of the forces that tenaciously hold existing behavior patterns in place.

Continue to work on our own transformation; share our struggles, as appropriate, with the leader and thus share our journeys.

Create an environment clearly supportive of the leader's new behaviors by providing the complementary behaviors required for the leader's efforts to be successful.

We should encourage leaders to share their efforts at changing their behavior with those affected by their behavior. Leaders should acknowledge the behavior and its effects and explain what they are trying to do about it. There may be initial cynicism about their sincerity, but if they are authentically struggling to transform, this will soon come across. Openness about the need to change generates further support.

By involving the immediate community in the transformation effort, leaders create their own additional internal commitment to implement and sustain new behaviors. Not only don't leaders want to fail after announcing their intentions, they also don't want to let down those who are being so supportive.

The individuals and groups affected by a leader's behavior must be open to the possibility of the leader changing. Too often there is a refusal to let go of past mistakes leaders have made. "I don't trust her because . . ." Courageous followers confront the group as well as the leader. Group members need to be willing to take another chance, to proceed with cautious open-mindedness, to not cynically dismiss the transformation effort before it begins or preordain its failure.

Even if we've been victimized by the leader, we need to support a genuine transformation effort. This is the heart of forgiveness—forgiving who someone once was, out of respect for who they are trying to become.

MODELING CHANGE FOR A LEADER

When a leader is engaged in transformation, old ways of doing things become insupportable and start to break down. The leader begins searching for new ways of doing things. Models become important.

Followers can sometimes provide those models. A follower is no more a paragon of exemplary behavior than a leader, but we each have our strengths. The leader models behavior that we learn from all the time; we can do the same for the leader. The most germane behavior we can model to help a leader transform is our own openness to transformation. And our openness to transformation begins by being willing to show our vulnerabilities.

We are not prone to showing vulnerabilities around leaders, nor are they prone to doing so around us. We are selected or hired to be competent, to have or generate answers, to be part of the solution. Yet if we feel we can never appear uncertain or vulnerable, we are telling our leaders they cannot be vulnerable either. Openness sets the stage for leaders and followers to engage in a genuine change process. We need to learn and, by our example, teach that some degree of shared vulnerability is necessary for transformation.

How do we model openness to change?

We can initiate discussions of sensitive topics about ourselves.

We can model soliciting personal feedback by showing genuine interest in how others perceive us.

We can voice our fears and not duck the subject when others raise their fears.

We can talk about the negative impact our behavior has on others and how we are trying to remedy that.

We can talk about both our successes and our setbacks with our own transformation efforts.

Modeling vulnerability is a real test of courage. It's risky. It can be turned on us. It can be overdone. But the alternative is stagnation behind rigid facades that we all work overtime to maintain.

MODELING EMPATHY

We can model any characteristic we possess or develop, but the most important one to model may be empathy. A leader must be able to empathize with real people and not just serve abstractions. Among the most abusive acts are those committed by leaders who passionately pursue revolutionary social goals, but are incapable of feeling or identifying with the pain of a single individual.

This anesthetized condition occurs more frequently among men. In many cultures boys are trained to repress their feelings, and they learn this lesson well. Its extreme manifestation occurs in men who gravitate to power out of a deep psychological need to deny their vulnerability. By contrasting their strength with the weakness of their victims, they stave off feeling vulnerable. Fear of feeling fear shuts down all feelings.

Because these individuals cannot experience their own feelings, they cannot identify with another's. The "other" can then be objectified and dehumanized, which sets the climate for inhumane acts to be perpetrated against them. This may not be the usual climate in which we live and work, but evidence of this condition exists all around us—in the daily news stories about rival gang gun fights, ethnic atrocities, and brutal civil wars. Someone is "leading" those acts and others are following.

While most of the situations we encounter will fall short of these extremes, it is the follower's imperative to help an "unfeeling" leader regain the ability to feel the pain of another human being. A follower's most available and powerful tool for doing this is his own feelings. It is a mistake for a follower whose leader is shut off from feelings to allow the leader to become the model for feeling-behavior in the group.

Instead, a courageous follower will model for the leader how to contact feelings and will demonstrate the difference between compassion and weakness. A follower must listen carefully to his feelings about the leader's words and actions, and report those feelings to the leader as he would describe visual events to a person who has lost his sight:

"That scares me because it lacks respect for basic human rights."

"I would feel betrayed if that action was directed at me."

"I feel disappointed hearing you say that and I think others will too."

"My trust would be severely shaken."

"Real people will experience real pain if that occurs."

"I feel outraged hearing you discuss people in those terms."

"I would cry if I found we were party to such an action."

Leaders who lack empathy are also chronically disdainful of others. They have lost touch with the actual conditions of the lives of their followers and the lives of those whom the organization serves. Disdainful leaders no longer understand the challenges followers face in getting their jobs done. They harp on lack of perfection and undermine the mutual respect needed to pursue a common purpose.

A transformational strategy is needed to increase empathy and bridge the gulf between the disdainful leader and others. The story of the monarch who disguises himself to roam among his subjects and find out what they really think and feel is applicable. Some organizations require senior executives to spend a week or two a year doing frontline jobs so they stay connected to the reality of what it takes to serve customers. Actually doing, not inspecting or critiquing, jobs at different levels of the organization can be eye-opening as to the skill required and the problems encountered. Disdain may rapidly transform into admiration and respect, or at least understanding.

Getting out in the field and talking to the end consumer of the organization's work—the trucker who drives the vehicles the company builds, the pensioner who depends on the services the agency provides, the family who is counting on the insurance company to come through for them—helps restore the loss of empathy that success and prominence sometimes breed.

Courageous followers can encourage leaders to agree that they and their closest followers take turns occasionally doing frontline jobs. As we gain prestige in tandem with our leaders, we are also susceptible to losing our empathy for others, and must periodically close the distance that arises between us and those we serve.

CONTAINING ABUSIVE BEHAVIOR

While modeling ways to change, followers may also need to help leaders contain abusive behavior until they can transform it. For example, a leader who screams needs to modify this behavior while working to transform the underlying causes. Otherwise, the bond between the leader, followers, and common purpose is severely weakened.

Anger is a potentially creative tool if it is not repressed nor allowed to get out of control. It can be used as an emotional sensor to detect something wrong that cannot yet be fully articulated. Learning to see repressed anger and invite its verbal expression can prevent the anger from reaching a boiling point where it becomes abusive.

But in leaders who display sudden, explosive anger, the emotional energy is so great that it demands physical release before the underlying situation can be verbalized and explored. A courageous follower coaching a leader in alternatives to abusive ranting might consider the following:

> Anger triggers the "fight or flight" mechanism; the adrenalin this pumps through the system must be released.

> In a person who slowly builds up anger, excess adrenalin can be drained by regular physical exercise; many people who work closely with leaders know what a difference exercise makes to their leaders' temperament.

> In leaders who become suddenly overwhelmed with anger, it is more difficult finding socially acceptable outlets for the adrenalin; behavior such as throwing things, fist banging, and hurling epithets intimidates others and is abusive.

> Ideally, mechanisms for releasing the anger would be used by the leader in private, but sometimes an otherwise highly regarded leader cannot exert the self-control to do this. In this case, it may help to have tools available for the leader's use when needed.

> While it may seem strange, it is far less intimidating behavior for a leader convulsed with anger to dissipate it by twisting a golf towel or squeezing a soft chair, while repeating a nondirective epithet such as "damn," than to verbally abuse followers. A quick walk around the block will further dampen the surge of stress hormones.

> In a quieter moment, the leader can explain why she is doing this; the objective is to release the physical energy without wounding people with verbal shrapnel and threatening behavior.

Efforts at transforming abuse are not a license to continue the abuse. Since abusive behavior is immature, when courageous followers set limits on what they will tolerate, it helps leaders contain the behavior. Containing abusive behavior buys leaders the time they need to explore the roots of the behavior and work through the transformation process.

POSITIVE REINFORCEMENT

Insights may occur in a flash, but this is rarely true of lasting transformation. Translating insights into new ways of relating to ourselves and others is usually a long, uneven process. Successful transformation is assisted by reinforcement when we are successful at changing a behavior and disconfirmation when we are not. Reinforcement and disconfirmation require an outside agent, and followers can perform this role for a leader. It will help to bear these principles in mind when providing reinforcement:

> **Constant correction erodes self-confidence.**
>
> **If leaders feel assaulted or harassed, they will wall themselves off from continued criticism to protect their self-esteem and ability to exercise power.**
>
> **It is far more important to acknowledge leaders when they display some of the desired behavior than it is to correct them because they have not effected all of it.**
>
> **Catching leaders in the act of "doing the right thing" helps them form a permanent memory of what the desired behavior looks and feels like.**
>
> **Acknowledging small, positive changes builds confidence about change itself and the rewards change brings.**

Disconfirmation is needed when appropriate, but we must make sure that we are even more quick to notice and acknowledge improvements.

COPING WITH RECURRING BEHAVIOR

When there are too few examples of a leader doing the right thing and too many of continuing the offending behavior, both disconfirmation and coping mechanisms are needed.

We'll find ourselves better prepared to give disconfirming feedback if we get the leader's agreement on our role:

"Would it help if I mention it if I observe you doing this again?"

If leaders agree intellectually that change is important, but for whatever reason are not actually making that change, they should be open to the group developing coping mechanisms to minimize the effect of their behavior. Coping mechanisms combine ways of empowering the group to behave functionally with consequences that disconfirm the leader's disruptive behavior. Examples include:

> **If the leader chronically comes to work at 10:00 a.m., she will not require staff who start at 8:00 a.m. to do support work in the evenings.**

> **If the leader bottlenecks communications that require her signature, staff will be empowered to take them off her desk after three days and sign for her.**

> **If the leader screams and abuses staff, they will get up and leave until she regains self-control.**

> **If the leader dominates meetings, she will put five dollars in a kitty for each statement that cuts off group input, as will anyone in the group who cuts off others.**

Agreed-upon consequences remove the feedback process from the verbal level and place it on the action level. This is important, as a follower may be reluctant to appear the nag by continuously harping on the recurring behavior.

Recognizing that there are consequences to behavior is a key element in the transformation process. Self-initiated consequences provide leaders with symbols of potentially harsher public consequences should their behavior remain unchanged. And agreed-upon coping mechanisms give followers a way of taking care of their needs and the needs of the organization while the leader works to improve.

REALISTIC EXPECTATIONS

The roots of the attitudes and behaviors we seek to transform may be planted in body memories formed long before we learned to ride a bicycle, and may last just as long as that remarkable piece of programming.

When we grow up speaking one language and learn another later in life, we will retain the accent of the first. Our mouth and tongue have learned to form certain shapes and continue to do so. We can reduce the accent, but not eliminate it. So it is with the core behaviors of our personality. It will help us remain supportive if we bear in mind a few things about transformation efforts:

Don't expect perfect responses; leaders are no more perfect than we are.

Expect to see more balance between strengths and weaknesses, not a total transformation of character.

Look for a shift in emphasis between competing values—perhaps more concern for the people and process and less for the outcome regardless of human costs.

Expect more consciousness of certain actions and the effects the actions have, not the immediate cessation of those actions.

Recognize that when individuals become aware of doing something "wrong," it is a precursor to their being able to check themselves and do it differently.

Anticipate regression under pressure; recognize it as a natural part of the learning cycle and an opportunity for further growth.

We can acknowledge our disappointment or anger when we see old behaviors still at work, but not let those feelings derail our support for the process. The courageous follower participates in transformation within the larger context of the group's mission and doesn't fixate on the failure to transform every detail and action. We are aiming for better balance and the ability to achieve the organization's purpose. These are realistic and important expectations.

PERSISTENCE

In transformation, as in virtually every human activity, persistence is often the difference between success and failure. If we do not persist, we "give up," and those who give up are no longer assuming responsibility for the situation. To a greater or lesser degree, they become alienated.

Alienation is not conducive to the growth of the follower, the leader, or the organization. An organization being hurt by a leader's dysfunctional behavior is further hurt by losing the committed energy of followers. The common purpose severely suffers.

There are many reasons that change may not be happening as quickly as we would like:

The timing may be wrong.

Distractions in the environment may overwhelm the effort.

The intervention may be inadequate; we may need to seek a second opinion, as we would in a deteriorating medical situation.

The consequences may still be too remote to provide motivation.

The effort may be undermined by actions from a more senior level or another influence.

Our own transformation may not be far enough along to serve as a catalyst for the leader's transformation.

For the leader and follower, as for any people in a relationship, commitment and stick-to-it-iveness are needed to overcome adversity and work out interpersonal difficulties.

When leaders try to improve an organization's awareness and behavior, they find many ways of sending their message throughout the organization. Customer-service campaigns, for example, run for years with training, speeches, newsletters, posters, videos, focus groups, reengineering processes, incentive programs, award ceremonies, and so on. When followers try to raise leaders' awareness and influence their choices, they may also need to find many ways of getting the message across. Transformation requires patience and determination, creativity and determination, determination and more determination.

A courageous follower's art is to persist without letting the effort deteriorate into a power struggle. The follower's need to make an impact cannot drive the process. The drivers must continue to be the common purpose and the welfare of the leader, the organization, and those the organization serves.

If we get haughty, if we become arrogant about the leader, we have become "hooked." Something in our own psyche, something of our own issues with power has been triggered. We can't lead the leader in areas we have not ourselves addressed. We would do better to work on these for a while rather than unproductively butt egos with the leader.

We must remember that more change may be happening under the surface than is apparent from the leader's visible behavior. The struggle is like hatching an egg—a lot of work is done inside the shell where others can't see it before the first cracks appear, let alone a hole large enough to step through. Just when we think we cannot reach this person, that she is not capable of change, she may make her breakthrough—darkness before the dawn. Just when we think we cannot make this relationship work, *we* may have our own breakthrough that unlocks it.

VALIDATION

When transformation occurs it should be acknowledged. We all believe we are good people. When that belief has been challenged and we have walked the difficult road of attempting to match reality with our beliefs, we deserve to hear about that as clearly as we heard about our flaws. This does not mean rewarding new behavior, which is somewhat manipulative and demeaning, but honoring it as a real achievement, a victory we can all appreciate. Nor does this mean validating transformation at the first sign of improvement, because premature validation can demotivate the leader. It does mean validating sustained change:

> "I'd like you to know how consistently I see you doing _____ ."

> "I want you to know I no longer experience _____ in our relationship and what a difference that has made."

> "In the last few months, I've felt better than ever about how we work together."

> "I've heard a lot of admiration from the field about how you _____ ."

> "In my estimation, the results we are now achieving are due in no small part to the change you've made in _____ ."

> "My hat's off to you. It took a lot of courage to do what you did."

While we may achieve many victories in our lives, genuine transformation is often the hardest and most precious. When we are close to a leader who has been transformed we should bear witness to that transformation, both to the leader and to the world. Validation helps strengthen the fibers of new patterns so they wear well through the fraying challenges that lie ahead.

6

THE COURAGE
TO LEAVE

MERGING AND SEPARATING are two of the most basic acts of life. At different stages of our lives and relationships we join or we leave others. From birth to death this is a profound act. In the middle there may be loves found and lost, loyalties given and withdrawn, positions occupied and abandoned.

Giving part of ourselves to another is a fundamental act of family, groups, and society. The ability to reclaim that part of ourselves is equally fundamental. Faced with the death of a beloved spouse, we need to find a way to again live without the other. Faced with an abusive spouse, we need to find a way to extricate ourselves from the damaging relationship and make our own way in the world. When we outgrow a group, or when it stagnates and we cannot rejuvenate it, or when it betrays our loyalty, we need to move on to other groups that can fill our needs and utilize our contributions.

Each of these acts requires courage. For better or worse, the known is predictable; the unknown is not. Can we succeed, or even survive, when we leave the familiar situation? We don't know until we try. There are many valid reasons for a courageous follower to separate from a leader, ranging from the benign to the life-threatening.

GROWTH

The most benign, natural reason to move on is growth. Leaders mentor us; we learn and grow. At some point we are ready to move from under their shadow. We are ready to seek other mentors, to test what we have learned, to serve in ways we have discovered we were meant to serve, or to explore what those ways might be.

We may admire or even love the leader. But it is time to go. It is time to better define ourselves independently, even if doing so proves to be preparation for returning to serve the leader and our common purpose in new ways.

As stewards of the purpose, we make detailed preparations to transfer responsibilities so that service to the leader and organization continues uninterrupted. We leave without a sudden rupture.

GROUP OPTIMIZATION

Group optimization is the reverse side of the coin of leaving for our personal growth; it means the leader and organization may need to grow. Sometimes a leader needs fresh input. The loyalty and experience of long-serving followers may be outweighed by a stasis of new ideas. A calcification of methods serves the common purpose poorly.

A time may come when we sense the organization's need for new blood. Or it is pointed out to us by others. A courageous follower acknowledges when this is true, recognizing that the right infusion can rejuvenate the leader and organization. The challenge is to accept this passage as a natural flow of life, not as a personal failing; to take advantage of the opportunity to examine our own needs and explore new ways to better meet these.

When members of a high-performance team separate for reasons of personal growth or group optimization, and then join or form other organizations, the original group doesn't die as much as it transforms into a living network. If the relationships have been kept healthy and the separation is done well, a new kind of power emerges from the bonds between people who are connected through their fields and across the disciplines.

EXHAUSTION

If we become exhausted, we lose our ability to serve the common purpose. If we have not managed ourselves well or are being used up by a leader, we may need to separate in order to reclaim and rejuvenate ourselves.

The nurturing a follower receives from a leader does not have to be equal to that which a follower gives a leader, but it must be present and meaningful. If it is not and we are unsuccessful at changing this, the self-responsible act may be to leave.

PRINCIPLED ACTION

Courageous followership is principled followership. If we have failed to serve the common purpose in some important way, we must be willing to resign the position given us in trust. If a leader is failing to serve the common purpose in some important way, and will not recognize or change this, courageous followers may need to tender their resignation as the only principled option available.

If the leader is not simply failing to serve the common purpose, but is using the organization's energy and resources in violation of its values, courageous followers become as committed to disempowering the leader as they were to supporting him.

Leaving on principle is a key act of followership that we will examine in this chapter. I know personally how difficult it can be. In my mid-thirties, I found that I had devoted a significant portion of my adult life to an organization and its leader that were increasingly at odds with my values and vision. Initially, I couldn't acknowledge my discomfort with the leader's actions. I manifested the conflict I felt through stress-induced illness. Only when I became persona non grata for participating in an internal reform effort did I confront the fact that it was truly time to separate.

But for some of my contemporaries in the organization, leaving wasn't enough. They felt it important to publicly oppose the organization's practices. Still others, who were also uncomfortable with the practices, felt duty-bound to stay with the organization and try to be change agents from within. This is a personal decision. There is not necessarily a moral imperative to choose one course or the other. But it is important that we make the decision consciously.

In this chapter we'll examine appropriate separation, the resources needed to bolster our courage to make necessary moves, the power contained in resignation, circumstances that warrant disavowing or opposing a leader, and moral strategies for those who decide they must stay despite values clashes with the leader.

Healthy followership is a conscious act of free will. When we no longer believe that what we are doing is the best thing or the right thing, we must consciously review our options and their respective consequences. Otherwise we are in danger of becoming automatons with a dulled sense of responsibility for our actions, who serve neither ourselves nor the leader and common purpose well.

DIFFICULTY OF SEPARATION

In a relationship between dynamic leaders and committed followers who share a common purpose, withdrawing support from a leader is a wrenching act. It is closer to the experience of divorce than it is to leaving one job for another. As in a divorce, it can take months to begin recovering from the experience and years to fully recover.

The leader won the loyalty of followers because of a shared commitment to a common purpose and of the many attractive attributes the leader brought to the pursuit of that purpose. Whether or not these attributes have been obscured by less attractive ones, the prospect of leaving can stir up conflicted feelings in the follower.

There are many scenarios in which separation is difficult. If a leader and organization are failing, the most painful loss may be that of our dreams, of the expectations we had for the organization, its cause, and our own future. We may need to mourn these losses in order to fully separate.

Fearing the loss of reflected power from the leader also causes reluctance to separate. We come to believe that our ability to live a meaningful life and maintain a sense of control over our destiny are dependent on the leader's fortune. We may need to rediscover our internal compass and our own power. Though some people will stop returning our phone calls and cease being supportive when we lose our reflected power, we'll soon discover the genuine relationships in our lives.

Sometimes we become overly specialized, having served a particular organization and leader for many years. We wonder how we will survive; who would want us if we leave? Sometimes we just lose the habit of how to live outside the organization. Followers working in intense environments that demand round-the-clock activity, such as senior political offices, advocacy groups, or start-up companies in highly competitive industries, are particularly prone to sacrificing time with their families and communities. They need to regain familiarity with living a balanced life.

Separation difficulty is ultimately a crisis of identity. We are no longer sure of who we are, independent of the organization. The organization forms an important part of our identity in an age when other institutions that traditionally have given people a sense of belonging have weakened. This is seen in its extreme form in cults, whose members cease belonging to any other unit in society and derive their identity nearly completely from cult membership. But the phenomenon is a widespread occurrence in less pathological forms: witness recent retirees or people whose jobs have been eliminated. Drawing our identity from involvement in an organization raises the emotional stakes of leaving.

Followers struggling with separation might ask themselves these questions:

Who am I on my own?

What do I believe?

What do I want?

Is the organization's purpose still my purpose?

Are there other ways to pursue this purpose?

What do I really need to survive?

What are my skills?

What else could I do with these skills?

What gives me satisfaction?

What would I be willing to take risks for?

Who are my real friends?

What do I owe the leader and the organization?

What do they owe me?

How can we discharge these obligations to each other?

Our identity is never really lost, just obscured. We are wise to maintain relationships and interests outside the organization, for their own sake as well as for their importance in retaining our independent identity. This will make leaving the leader and organization considerably easier when the time comes to do so.

FINANCIAL CONTINGENCIES

Most followers are not independently wealthy. The financial factors involved in leaving are often as weighty as the emotional factors. If leaving is a considered decision made mutually with the leader, we usually have little financial problem making the transition. But we will also examine a range of circumstances in which the separation may be sudden. If our principles require us to resign or to take a confrontational stand that may lead to dismissal, financial factors come into play, sometimes decisively.

If we don't have financial contingency plans in place, our courage may be offset by our responsibilities. Many of us are contributing to the support of a family. Some are the sole support. Few of us can weather prolonged unemployment or a dramatic pay cut without seriously affecting our standard of living. Yet staying in a position for financial reasons, when doing so no longer serves us or the common purpose, can psychologically and spiritually exact as great a toll as unemployment does.

Particularly if the environment has become abusive, we can experience a terrible internal values conflict: on the one hand intellectual honesty, moral integrity, and self-esteem cry for us to speak the truth as we see it. On the other hand responsibility for our family, investment in our career, and yearning for security act as restraining forces against our speaking candidly. It is healthy for followers to develop financial contingency plans so that fear of losing our position never prevents us from speaking the truth about ourselves or our leaders. Paradoxically, such plans are also healthy for leaders because their existence improves the prospects of leaders receiving honest feedback.

Financial contingency plans might include:

money in the bank that enables us to "walk away" and still meet our financial obligations until we can reestablish ourselves;

agreement with a spouse or partner to support each other if one of us must leave our employment for reasons of conscience, until we can find or develop another opportunity;

establishing an ample line of credit while we are in a strong position to do so;

continuing to live within our former means when we are elevated to a higher position, so we can afford to lose that position;

staying visible in our field, to improve our chances for a successful lateral move if we leave the organization;

maintaining a sideline business, hobby, or other marketable skills that we can further develop if we must leave our field;

negotiating a contract that clearly spells out terms of severance we can live with.

Every generation observes the idealism and risk-taking of youth replaced by the pragmatic conservatism of age. As we age, we usually have more to lose. Our risk-taking is replaced by another type of courage—the courage to be responsible for others. If we can put financial contingency plans in place, we are in a stronger position to remain pragmatic without sacrificing our ideals.

OFFERING TO RESIGN

While separation from an organization may be a long, well-considered process, resignation based on principles is often abrupt. We can resign because of our own breach of trust or in protest of the leader's. We'll examine the former situation first.

From the day courageous followers assume a position of trust close to a prominent leader, they must be prepared to resign if they break that trust. Leaders and their teams are trusted to vigorously pursue the common purpose within the framework of community and organizational values. Even the appearance of having broken that trust may require resignation. It is best to mentally prepare for this eventuality from the start. When circumstances demanding resignation occur, we usually have little time and scant mental and emotional resources to think things through.

The need to offer our resignation in the face of a breach of trust develops out of a sense of why we are there and whom we serve. Resigning can be a statement of commitment to the common purpose and an act of confirming community values. It is not egoless, but ego-respecting—we have too much respect for ourselves, the leader, and the organization to be found writhing out of our moral obligations.

Under these circumstances, a resignation needs to be tendered quickly to make an effective moral statement. If it is offered belatedly, it appears to be what it is—bowing to pressure—rather than an honorable recognition of the real or perceived breach of trust. An effective resignation can itself be a redemptive act. At this stage, considerations about our own welfare and what we will do next are inappropriate. Of course these anxieties are present, but they are outside the imperative of our decision.

On the other hand, a resignation is not offered lightly. It is not an appropriate response to every mistake. We cannot demand perfection of ourselves any more than we can demand it of our leaders. Organizations and individuals pursue their purpose and meet their objectives by doing and failing and learning and doing. Nor does a courageous follower resign to avoid responsibility for cleaning up a mess. It may take more courage to stay on the scene and spend years unraveling the consequences of our actions than it does to leave.

Sometimes offering to resign is protective of the leader, showing respect for his values, and helping distance him from a debacle he did not cause, from actions he did not sanction. A resignation can be a courageous act that clarifies accountability. But "taking the fall" for a leader obscures accountability and may not serve the common purpose well.

Early in their relationship with a leader, courageous followers should establish criteria for resignation:

> **Under what circumstances must I resign? What types of activities would violate the core values of this organization and its community?**

> **Under what circumstances should I consider resigning? What activities would appear to violate the organization's values, even if they represent poor judgment rather than betrayal of trust?**

> **Under what circumstances should I hold my ground? When would it serve the organization to do so, even if it hurts me or the leadership?**

Thinking through these questions can clarify values and formulate guidelines for future actions. This clarity may prevent real or perceived violations of trust from occurring.

If it is appropriate to offer to resign, the courageous follower approaches the leader with speed and deliberation. If the leader concurs with the follower's decision to resign, they decide together how to announce and implement the decision. The resignation becomes a final team effort that confirms the organization's values, minimizes disruption to the organization's pursuit of its purpose, and respects the overall contributions of the follower.

THREATENING TO RESIGN

We must be as prepared to resign in protest of a leader's actions that threaten the common purpose or violate the community's values as we are prepared to resign due to our own actions. The implicit power to withdraw support is one of the powers that permits a follower to influence events. It is always present and is usually unstated. In organizations where followers have served leaders for a protracted time, the follower's continued loyalty may be taken for granted. If a leader does not treat seriously the need for change, a follower may need to exercise that power to withdraw support through an explicit warning.

Not only must we tell leaders *how* we feel, but we must tell them how *intensely* we feel about issues that concern us. In collections of people that are not true groups, individuals will just leave if they are discontented. They do not engage in uncomfortable, energy-demanding confrontation. In a true group, members will speak up clearly and forcefully before exercising the option to leave.

The warning of impending resignation, if not used lightly, is one of the legitimate ways to voice the depth of our concern. If we are viewed as a loyal follower, the fact that we would consider leaving over the issue strengthens the impact of what we are saying.

> "I must advise you this is a decision I cannot live with. I believe it places our people at unnecessary and unacceptable risk."

> "I need to be clear about this. I will not be able to go along with that approach as I believe it violates our basic principles."

> "If we cannot agree to modify our position, regretfully I will need to resign as I cannot be party to it."

When fundamental values conflict, when core policy differences are not treated seriously, or when transformation efforts deteriorate to lip service, threatening to withdraw support is an important moral tool. If we communicate that the potential consequences of these conditions include our resignation, we may elevate an issue so it is viewed with sufficient gravity for change to occur. And if we don't succeed, the situation has been unmistakably clarified and can inform our decision to stay or leave.

THE DILEMMA OF
THE "UNREASONABLE" LEADER

The "unreasonable" man or woman is sometimes said to be the primary agent of change in a culture. Reasonable people adapt to their surroundings; unreasonable individuals change those surroundings to better suit their needs. The strength of an unreasonable leader is the ability to think outside the current paradigm and envision entirely new possibilities. This is the leader who comes in and turns a place on its ear. Suddenly everything feels different. Expectations are astronomically higher. Stability is not valued. Change is initiated everywhere. Old assumptions are flushed into the open and challenged. The pace is significantly accelerated. Relationships are altered. The universe is no longer as we knew it.

"Unreasonable" leaders can make even courageous followers uncomfortable with the scope and rate of change. We may resist such leaders and be fearful of the consequences of their actions. Yet these may be the very actions that the organization needs to survive or to create breakthroughs. In our inability to see beyond our paradigm, to appreciate the leader's prescience, to cope with the discomfort created, we may be tempted to withdraw our support though the leader fully deserves it.

How can we differentiate between our inertia and fears and our legitimate concerns for the organization in the hands of an iconoclastic leader? Once again, values and purpose must be our guiding lights:

> Are the core values of the community and organization being respected? (Not the peripheral values, but the core values.)

> Are peripheral values that do not forward the common purpose being challenged? In a social service agency, for example, going easy on staff and not pushing them may have become a value that lowered the quantity and quality of badly needed services.

Are the twin tests of honesty and decency being met? They important barometers of the respect being shown for core values; if the leader is communicating honestly and people are treated decently, even when they have to be moved aside to get the job done, power is being used not abused.

Is the flurry of actions being taken geared to achieve the common purpose and not some other agenda of the leader's?

Are the risks being taken justified? The "unreasonable" leader may take high risks, as leaders sometimes must, but those high risks should outweigh the risks of inaction or "safe" action.

Are the processes of group input respected while being accelerated, so the organization becomes a stronger team, more capable of achieving its purpose over time?

If values are being respected and the purpose is being served, we can get aboard the leader's express. If they are not, his actions must be challenged. Brilliance and dynamism without strong, decent values are untrustworthy vehicles for power, regardless of their expediency.

VALUES REVIEW

The actions of a leader who is abusing power can be so at odds with his proclaimed values that cognitive dissonance prevents us from fully registering the discrepancies. But we do experience discomfort at the perimeters of our awareness and must try to pay attention to it.

Whether we become aware of the values conflict gradually, or because of some isolated episode that assaults our sense of decency, this awareness must trigger a hard review of the leader's actual values. To conduct a values review, we can:

Compile a list of our own values.

Compile a list of the leader's stated values that we share.

Compile a list of recent actions taken by the leader.

Review which actions support our values and those the leader purports to share, and which conflict with them.

After completing the values review, we must make a decision:

If the leader's actions largely support our values, and do not egregiously violate any of them, we should continue our support.

If the leader's actions largely conflict with our values, or egregiously violate core values, we must be prepared to withdraw our support.

The critical differentiation in this process is between statements and actions. Leaders who violate values attempt to obfuscate the record with explanations. As long as we believe a leader is serving the common purpose, we would like to believe those explanations. We are prone to deny abusive acts. We may even become apologists for them. A hard look at actions clarifies the situation.

FOLLOWER
SELF-EXAMINATION

When courageous followers believe that neither the organization's values nor its purpose are being served well by the leader, and they are considering withdrawing support, they should also examine themselves before acting.

In many organizational cultures, colleagues sympathize with us if we gripe to them about the leader. Friends and family do, too. We can mistake this as strong support for our views. To ensure our actions will benefit the organization and those it serves, we must seek good counsel just as we encourage our leaders to do. To help us discern right-motivated action:

We can ask for guidance from our peers, for feedback on how they perceive our reactions to the leader.

We should choose these peers for their diversity and honesty, not just for their history of supporting us.

We should frame our concerns in a nonincendiary way, so the healthy act of examination isn't held against us if we decide we are not justified in withdrawing support.

We should not ask for our peers' views in order to manipulate them into our position or reduce our own responsibility for our decision.

We want as much objectivity as we can get, not to replace our inevitable subjectivity but to test it.

We must be as open to challenge as we wish our leader to be; we must try to behave in the way that we are concerned he does not.

If peers advise against withdrawing support because they feel we are off the mark, involved in our own issues with authority, power grabbing, or failing to see the larger picture, their advice must be taken seriously. If they caution not to withdraw support because of the potential personal consequences, courageous followers may elect to ignore this advice and put values and purpose first.

THE RESPONSIBILITY TO WITHDRAW SUPPORT

The bottom line of followership is that we are responsible for our decision to continue or not to continue following a leader. Even *in extremis*, we have the choice of supporting an anathema to our values or not. This is the Nuremberg trials principle. The fact that we are following orders absolves us from nothing. Of course this choice is made in the context of our full values structures. Competing values, such as love for and responsibility to our family, may make the choice difficult, even excruciating, but we always have choices and are responsible for the ones we make.

If we have honestly examined ourselves and energetically worked to help a leader transform, yet still find a significant gap between a leader's actions and our core values, we have to give very serious consideration to withdrawing our support. Commitment is central to a relationship, but does not necessarily bind us if the relationship is stagnant or destructive despite our energetic efforts to improve it.

When the relationship principles examined in this guide fail to help a leader maintain a balanced use of power, the difficulty may stem from psychological roots that are beyond the reach of a follower's influence. It is critical that we recognize when our ability to influence a situation has been exceeded, when withdrawal is the appropriate course.

The duty to withdraw support increases in proportion to the egregiousness of the violation of values and our proximity to the leader. Our responsibility as close followers is great because often only the inner circle sees the leader's true values at an early stage; others may still see only the public persona. We can protect a values-deficient leader and allow him to amass power, or we can strip away the camouflage we are providing.

When courageous followers withdraw support from a leader, it will help to bear in mind the following:

> If we are among the first in a group to withdraw support, we will need the conviction of our values, confidence in our powers of observation, and the courage to maintain our isolated position.

> When we separate from a leader we must also question whether the common purpose we shared with the leader is valid.

> If the purpose is valid, we must examine our commitment to it independent of our relationship with the leader and identify other ways, consistent with our commitment, of pursuing that purpose.

> We will add to the emotional and material cost of separation if we continue supporting a cause out of unexamined habit, or abandon a cause close to our heart.

> If we leave and later events prove we were wrong about the leader, we should use the experience to learn more about our relationships with leaders, but we should never berate ourselves for having had the courage to act on our convictions.

When we withdraw support, we may need to come to terms with many things, including why we gave our support for as long as we did, what actions we took in the name of the cause, and our sense of loss and regret. None of this is easy, but it is far preferable to compounding the situation by lacking the courage to withdraw from it.

WHEN LEADERS MUST BE DISAVOWED

The decision to withdraw support from a leader does not automatically require disavowing that leader. Followers may simply decide there are more important purposes and more values-centered leaders to support, or that they are ready to test their own leadership abilities. We can withdraw amicably without detailing our reasons. This is the most common way of leaving. Resumes and references, if not relationships, stay intact.

There are circumstances, however, when followers have further obligations. When a leader's actions seriously endanger the organization or community, silent withdrawal is inappropriate. We need to draw public scrutiny to those actions. When respect for human life, for the welfare of children, for the rule of law, or any other basic values are violated, a line is crossed. Public disavowal is a tool for disempowering abusive leaders.

In order to disavow a leader, courageous followers must first disavow themselves of the belief that the situation will improve. Abusive leaders use words freely to buy time, to escape detection, and to amass power. We can only believe actions. Unless checked, leaders who abuse their closest followers, or others, will escalate the abuses in proportion to the power they amass. If the abuse is not weeded out at germination, it will grow and strangle rivals, followers, and bystanders alike.

When a leader's actions violate basic human decency, a courageous follower should consider the following gradations of response:

> The first incident or suggestion of violating basic human values
> must be energetically challenged.

> If a second incident occurs, it must be responded to with a clear
> statement of the intention to withdraw all support should it reoc-
> cur in any form. (If, in extreme cases, announcing that intention
> would jeopardize the follower's safety, it is best to proceed as if a
> third incident had occurred.)

> Repeated incidents should be met by withdrawing support and by
> public exposure. In this case, followers are wise to document
> their claims so they cannot be easily discredited.

> If followers cannot obtain documentation or corroboration for all
> their claims, but can for one claim, they should focus public
> attention on this point; one irrefutable demonstration of a
> leader's corruption is more powerful than many refutable charges.

Once we formally leave the organization, restraints on speech are lifted
and we can communicate more forcefully to a broader audience. Whatever
power we possessed by being close to a leader can now be directed to disavowing the violation of basic human values we have witnessed or perhaps
even contributed to.

EVIL BEHAVIOR

Any behavior falls somewhere along a spectrum of intensity for that type
of activity. The study of statistics tells us that the distribution of intensities
within a group always forms a familiar bell-shaped curve. Most people
display similar intensity of behavior, and form the top of the bell.
Diminishing numbers display lesser or greater intensities as we move
toward the extremes. About 2.5 percent approach either extreme and
fewer than .2 percent fall at either extreme itself.

Thus, most people are "averagely" good or bad, a handful stand out in either direction, and a tiny few are saintly or bedeviled. Because we so rarely encounter such extreme behavior, we may discount it. On the good-evil spectrum, we do so at great peril. As rare as it may be, extremely evil behavior does exist, and if not recognized and dealt with for what it is, will cause great suffering.

Evil acts are devoid of empathy for the suffering of others. They are only concerned with what the perpetrator gets out of the act. If the perpetrator benefits from or simply enjoys the victim's suffering, that is all that matters. There have been many attempts to explain the root of evil, but we seem no closer now to understanding or eradicating its roots than were ancient cultures. We can, however, observe the manifestations of evil and act to stop its progression. A willful leader who achieves his goals by harming others is on a narcissistic road away from decency. A leader who is allowed to act with indifference to the suffering of others is on a trajectory to extreme corruption of power.

Leaders who plan and commit evil acts usually mask them from the broader public until they have accumulated enough power to flaunt the behavior. Thus, fighting evil is like fighting a fire: it is better to contain it early than to wait until it is out of control and consuming everything in its path. Evil is best fought from within an organization by courageous followers close enough to the leader to see behind the public mask. We are the firebreak.

Evil is stoked and fanned by followers who abandon their empathy with the suffering of others, either through fear or through seduction by a leader who has lost his empathy. Followers who commit evil acts are not necessarily evil people. They may be under powerful pressure to perform these acts. Implicitly or explicitly, they have been promised personal gain for conforming and threatened with personal harm for not conforming. Because their peers are under the same pressure, these acts begin to appear normal. This is how millions of people came to support a Ku Klux Klan, a Nazi regime, or a Bosnian "ethnic cleansing." We must be vigilant against starting down the slippery slope of evil behavior:

The very first time we are pressured to commit an evil act, we will experience discomfort; an inner voice protests against it.

We must listen to this inner voice and recognize that it is more valid than the voice of our peers or leader and, with profound courage, must draw a line then and there.

If we do not listen to this inner voice, it will speak again when we actually commit the act; it may even scream in revulsion.

This may be our last opportunity to listen to the voice; if we do not listen now, we will need to smother it, anesthetize ourselves, and deny our deeds in order to live with them.

At that point we will become indistinguishable from an evil person.

When confronted with evil behavior we must not rationalize it, we must not hide in the false safety of the group, we must not stifle our internal screams in the silence of our peers. With the brightest searchlight we can find or build, we must expose the behavior against standards of basic human decency. We must become imbued with, and personally model, a revulsion at evil behavior. We must never underestimate it. We must not behave normally in its presence. The world continues to be littered with corpses, the victims of evil behavior. If we cannot help the perpetrators of evil to restrain and transform their behavior, we must use our power to expose, shun, and isolate them.

WHEN LEADERS
MUST BE OPPOSED

There is a large step between disavowing a leader and actively opposing him. When disavowing a leader, a follower is casting light on the leader's actions in the court of public opinion and leaving it to the corrective mechanisms of the organization or society to respond.

When courageous followers choose to actively oppose a leader, they themselves mobilize available mechanisms for disempowering the leader. When attention has been called to evil behavior and the corrective mechanisms of society respond too slowly or indifferently, courageous followers may feel responsible for firing them up. The police captain who brutally beats suspects, the politician who abrogates the legitimate constitution, the executive who orders a toxic-waste coverup, the zealot who commits arson to preserve his community's "racial purity," each deserve to be vigorously opposed.

Of course there are risks to opposing venality. The obvious risk is retaliation by leaders who are being opposed. There are also psychological risks. While these will not dissuade courageous followers, we should be aware of them:

Followers may become obsessed with opposing the leader and expend all their energy on efforts to stop him.

Followers who become obsessed run the risk of themselves disregarding basic human values in pursuit of their obsession.

Followers who become obsessed will pay a heavy price in their personal lives, as obsession is the destroyer of balance.

If followers were victimized by the leader they may wind up paying twice, once by the victimization and once by the obsession to stop it from happening to others.

This price may be the cost of disempowering evil, but it is a greater victory if followers pursue their goal with determination rather than obsession.

The antidote to obsession is generating as much energy toward the positive ideals we are trying to realize as toward the source of evil we are trying to stop.

A good example of a vigorous and balanced opposition to evil is a Klanwatch organization in the South that recognized it was becoming obsessed with exposing neofascist groups. In order to correct this, the organization initiated a project to teach tolerance in schools as a positive balance to its aggressive litigation program. If a follower's opposition is balanced, energetic, skillful, and timely, she can become the catalyst that triggers society's mechanisms for broadly exposing the abuse and preventing its recurrence. At this point the follower has transformed herself and become an opposition leader.

The most difficult and dangerous situation occurs when the abuse of power is violent and society's legal mechanisms for correcting it have been corrupted by the abusers. Opposition must be bold and imaginative to counter the use of violent force by mobilizing the overwhelming force of public opinion against it. We have watched the mixed successes of this type of opposition in Moscow and Beijing in recent years. Electronic media, which can focus the whole world's attention on an abuse of power, may be shifting the advantage to courageous followers and opposition leaders.

The gravest choice a courageous follower turned opposition leader makes is whether to use force to counter abusive lethal force. By doing so we risk escalating violence and suffering. Nonviolent resistance has always been a brave and morally unimpeachable response. But can we condemn the followers who tried to stop Hitler's carnage by concealing a bomb in a briefcase under the table at which Hitler sat? Few of us would condemn that act. We mourn that it failed! But it is rare when the case is so clear cut. Using violence to counter violence is a terrible, slippery slope. In almost all cases it, too, becomes abusive—the ultimate lose-lose situation.

When followers universally and unyieldingly oppose violent leaders while they are still vulnerable, we can avoid desperate situations in which we entertain opposing violent force with force.

PROTECTING YOURSELF

While few situations become as grave as that discussed above, it is not uncommon for a follower who disavows or opposes a leader to pay in some way. If leaders are deeply insecure and vindictive, they may retaliate for simply suggesting that they review their behavior or policies.

Courageous followers may need to come "armed" with "weapons" of their own—information, allies, bylaws, legal representation—that make the price of retaliating too high, and make cooperating with efforts to reform a situation more attractive. The best protection for abusive leaders is darkness and secrecy; our protection is light and documentation.

Followers are in a stronger position when they are insulated from formal retribution. Public officials appointed for fixed terms, educators with tenure, workers whose union will shield them from retaliatory demotion, staff who have accrued enough years of service for full retirement benefits, all enjoy some protection and are more prone to challenge leadership policies or practices with which they disagree. We would do well to try to create some of this insulation in our own lives. Contingency plans might include:

> obtaining strong written references, for use in a future employment search or court proceeding, before publicly opposing a leader;

> keeping detailed documentation of our activities and those of the leader to support our claims and refute retaliatory charges made about us;

> developing media relations who will be interested in our story when we are ready to tell it;

> affiliating with groups that will support us emotionally, legally, and financially if we oppose the leader's practices;

> making arrangements with friends or relatives to care for our families if a confrontation with the leader risks their physical or emotional safety.

Regardless of contingency arrangements, if we make the decision to visibly oppose a leader, our lives will be severely impacted. We will find ourselves under enormous stress. The least endearing parts of our personality may become more pronounced under this stress. At the time we most need support, we may drive it away.

It is important to be emotionally prepared for this and to prepare our support system. We need to confide in our family, friends, and colleagues. We need to give them a chance to be part of our decision-making process. When we call on them to stand by us, they will not feel they are being dragged into something without consultation. We must ground ourselves in the deepest sense of purpose and the highest values we have, so we can face whatever ordeal awaits us with grace rather than bitterness.

IF WE DECIDE TO STAY

Despite the moral demand to leave, a follower may choose to stay—the price of leaving may simply be too high. Courage is not absolute. We cannot judge another for making this choice unless we ourselves have faced it.

If we decide to stay, we may justify our decision on the grounds that if all the "moderate" people in the organization left, it would only become more extreme and harmful. There is some functional truth to this. It can require courage to remain in an organization whose values we do not share and whose excesses we intend to curb. It is a very unpleasant experience to continue dealing with people whose style and activities we abhor. But if our departure leaves them freer to abuse power, there is a moral argument to be made for staying.

If we make the choice to stay we must be prepared for several things:

We must accept moral and legal responsibility for the tacit or actual support we are giving to the abuse.

We can never claim before a legal or moral court that "we had no choice."

We must take incremental action at every opportunity to diminish the abuses and the impact they have on their victims.

We must take bold action to reform the organization when the moment for change presents itself and our stand can make a difference.

In its own way, the decision to stay as a moderating force is filled with as much risk as the decision to leave. We are a "fifth column" in hostile territory. Staying in the face of morally repugnant behavior is a questionable course for which the follower may pay with peace of mind, or worse. As is true for all moral decisions, it must be made with the greatest self-honesty we can manage.

EPILOGUE

THE WHOLESOME USE OF POWER does not assure success in achieving objectives, but is in itself success.

Both the common purpose and our integrity are served when core values guide us. The exercise of power presumes the hope for success and the willingness to risk failure, but a values-centered use of power assures that even if goal-achievement failures occur, they will not be compounded by failures of human decency.

The rewards of the balanced leader-follower relationship are the rewards of all healthy relationships—honest struggle, growth, mutual admiration, and even love. A reward of the wholesome use of power is the opportunity to witness improvements in the lives of those we serve. When leaders and followers fulfill their respective roles, they give each other the gift of being able to serve well. This service adds meaning to our lives.

Courage is a prerequisite to healthy relationships and a fulfilling life. Courageous leaders and followers working together sow seeds; when circumstances do not let them reap the harvest themselves, they leave the soil enriched by their integrity and commitment for the next planting.

MEDITATION ON FOLLOWERSHIP

FOR ME, BECOMING A COURAGEOUS FOLLOWER, like becoming a good human being, is both a daily and a life-long task. Visualizing a desired state helps to realize it. I share this meditation as one visualization of the state I aspire to. You may want to refer to it from time to time.

> **I am a steward of this group and share responsibility for its success.**

> **I am responsible for adhering to the highest values I can envision.**

> **I am responsible for my successes and failures and for continuing to learn from them.**

> **I am responsible for the attractive and unattractive parts of who I am.**

> **I can empathize with others who are also imperfect.**

As an adult, I can relate on a peer basis to other adults who are the group's formal leaders.

I can support leaders and counsel them, and receive support and counsel from them.

Our common purpose is our best guide.

I have the power to help leaders use their power wisely and effectively.

If leaders abuse power, I can help them change their behavior.

If I abuse power, I can learn from others and change my behavior.

If abusive leaders do not change their behavior, I can and will withdraw my support.

By staying true to my values, I can serve others well and fulfill my potential.

Thousands of courageous acts by followers can, one by one, improve the world.

Courage always exists in the present. What can I do today?

SELECT
BIBLIOGRAPHY

EPIGRAPH ON PAGE xi

The quote is from Baldesar Castiglione, *The Book of the Courtier*, translated by Charles S. Singleton (New York: Anchor Books, Doubleday & Co., 1959).

PREFACE

The information about the holocaust comes largely from two sources: Dr. Louis S. Snyder, *Encyclopedia of the 3rd Reich* (New York: Paragon House, 1989); and The United States Holocaust Memorial Museum, Washington, D.C.

CHAPTER 1

THE COMMON PURPOSE AND CORE VALUES

For vivid historical studies of the relationships among leaders, followers, and purposes, I recommend Gary Wills, *Certain Trumpets: The Call of Leaders* (New York: Simon & Schuster, 1994).

WHO DOES A FOLLOWER SERVE?

An extensive examination of how the roles of servant and leader, or servant and follower, can be fused is found in Robert K. Greenleaf, *Servant Leadership: A Journey into the Nature of Legitimate Power and Greatness* (New York: Paulist Press, 1977).

For a comparably rich examination of service and the appropriate use of power, see Peter Block, *Stewardship: Choosing Service Over Self-Interest* (San Francisco: Berrett-Koehler, 1993).

POWER IN THE LEADER-FOLLOWER RELATIONSHIP

I found a compelling discussion on the power to choose how we react—even in the horrific environment of a concentration camp—in Victor Frankl, *Man's Search for Meaning* (New York: Washington Square Press, 1959, 1984).

COURAGE OF THE FOLLOWER

For a profound and beautiful exploration of courage displayed before senior executives, read David Whyte, *The Heart Aroused: Poetry and the Preservation of the Soul in Corporate America* (New York: Currency Doubleday, 1994). The chapter "Fire in the Voice: Speaking Out at Work" is especially powerful.

FINDING EQUAL FOOTING WITH THE LEADER

I drew on a moving account of helping fellow sentient beings, regardless of their formal relationship to us, that I found in Ram Dass and Paul Gorman, *How Can I Help? Stories and Reflections on Service* (New York: Alfred A. Knopf, 1987).

CHAPTER 2

INTRODUCTION TO THE COURAGE
TO ASSUME RESPONSIBILITY

For the most serious discussion I have found on the responsibility of followers, and for a good instrument to measure yourself by, see Robert E. Kelley, *Power of Followership: How to Create Leaders People Want to Follow and Followers Who Lead Themselves* (New York: Double Currency, 1991).

ELICITING FEEDBACK

This book provides detailed process help on soliciting feedback from others: Dr. Mardy Grothe and Dr. Peter Wylie, *Problem Bosses: Who They Are and How to Deal with Them* (New York: Fawcett Crest, 1987).

SELF-MANAGEMENT

For an in-depth approach to improving personal organization, see Kerry Gleeson, *The Personal Efficiency Program: How to Get Organized to Do More Work in Less Time* (New York: John Wiley & Sons, Inc., 1994).

TESTING IDEAS

For a dynamic view of using pilots to test ideas, see Tom Peters, *Thriving on Chaos: A Handbook for a Management Revolution* (New York: Alfred A. Knopf, 1987).

CHAPTER 3

PRESENTING OPTIONS

A thorough approach for examining assumptions is presented in Stephen D. Brookfield, *Developing Critical Thinkers* (San Francisco: Jossey-Bass, 1987).

A comprehensive process for situation appraisal, problem analysis, and decision analysis is contained in Charles H. Kepner and Benjamin B. Tregoe, *The New Rational Manager* (New Jersey: Princeton Research Press, 1981).

I learned the rule of generating three options to assist in making ethical choices from Michael Josephson, The Josephson Institute of Ethics, Marina del Rey, California.

MANAGING CRISES
For a comprehensive review of preparing for crises, refer to Ian L. Miroff and Thierry C. Pauchant, *Transforming the Crisis-Prone Organization* (San Francisco: Jossey-Bass, 1992).

WHEN THE LEADER IS ILL
I drew on a fascinating treatise on the rarely examined subject of illness in leaders by Jerrold M. Post and Robert S. Robins, *The Captive King and His Captive Court: The Psychopolitical Dynamics of the Disabled Leader and His Inner Circle*. It is a paper presented to the American Political Science Association, September 1987.

CHAPTER 4

INVITING CREATIVE CHALLENGE
For a marvelous discussion of how to create group norms that encourage people to speak out without fear, see Kathleen D. Ryan and Daniel K. Oestreich, *Driving Fear Out of the Workplace* (San Francisco: Jossey-Bass, 1991).

While writing this book I participated in a stimulating program that demonstrated how to create an environment that encourages truly creative thinking. It is called the Mind-Free Program, developed by Kathleen Logan Prince and George M. Prince of Weston, Massachusetts.

OVERCOMING GROUPTHINK
The major work on this subject has been done by Irving L. Janis, *Groupthink, Psychological Studies of Policy Decisions and Fiascoes* (Boston: Houghton Miflin Company, 1972, 1982).

CHALLENGING THE USE OF LANGUAGE

The following book contains an important discussion on the power of language; it examines the problems of German psychotherapy patients whose families wouldn't talk about their role in World War II: *The Collective Silence*, edited by Barbara Heimannsberg and Christoph Schmidt (San Francisco: Jossey-Bass, 1992).

LEADERS WHO SCREAM

For a detailed process on how to comport oneself in the face of out-of-control screaming, listen to the section about bullying bosses on the tape by Robert Bramson, *Coping with Difficult Bosses* (New York: Simon and Schuster Audio, 1992).

CHAPTER 5

THE PROCESS OF PERSONAL TRANSFORMATION

A comprehensive and scholarly overview of the basic principles and processes of human psychological change is contained in Michael J. Mahoney, *Human Change Processes* (New York: Basic Books, a division of HarperCollins, 1991).

THE FOLLOWER'S ROLE

The literature on codependency contains important experience for those supporting a transformation process. The book I found most helpful as a resource is Melody Beattie, *Codependent No More: How to Stop Controlling Others and Start Caring for Yourself*, (San Francisco: HarperSanFrancisco, a division of HarperCollins, 1987).

THE FOLLOWER AS CATALYST; DENIAL AND JUSTIFICATION OF BEHAVIOR; IDENTIFYING TRANSFORMATION RESOURCES

The most important work I am aware of on the practical application of personal development to executive performance problems is Robert E.

Kaplan, *Beyond Ambition: How Driven Managers Can Lead Better and Live Better* (San Francisco: Jossey-Bass, 1991).

MODELING CHANGE FOR A LEADER
There is an interesting chapter on "Modeling Behavior: Helping Your Boss to Learn" in William P. Anthony, *Managing Your Boss* (New York: AMA-COM, American Management Associations, 1983).

MODELING EMPATHY
For one of the most profound discussions on denying vulnerability by victimizing others, see Ernst Becker, *Escape from Evil* (New York: The Free Press, a division of MacMillan Publishing Co., 1975).

CHAPTER 6

THREATENING TO RESIGN; IF WE DECIDE TO STAY
The original, brilliant thinking on this subject is found in the following book, which examines economic, political, and moral phenomena: Albert O. Hirschman, *Exit, Voice and Loyalty: Responses to Decline in Firms, Organizations, and States* (Cambridge: Harvard University Press, 1970).

For a derivative but illustrative complement to Hirschman, see the chapter "Quitting on Principle" in Warren Bennis, *Why Leaders Can't Lead* (San Francisco: Jossey-Bass, 1989).

EVIL BEHAVIOR
I'm sure that there are endless books describing statistical distribution, but as a nonstatistician I have used a book by Derek Rowntree, *Statistics Without Tears: A Primer for Non-Mathematicians* (New York: Charles Scribner's Sons, 1981).

For a hard look at the phenomenon of group evil, read the chapter "My Lai: An Examination of Group Evil" in M. Scott Peck, *People of the Lie: The Hope for Healing Human Evil* (New York: Simon & Schuster, A Touchstone Book, 1983).

INDEX

Responsibility, 3–4; for breaking rules, 46–47; for changing organizational mind-set, 48; courage to assume, 6, 33–50; for eliciting feedback, 38; for family support, 154–155; for group culture, 45–46; for improving processes, 49–50; for influence, 11–13; literature on, 181; and passion, 43–44; for personal growth, 39; for self, 36; for self-assessment, 36–37; for self-care, 41–42; for self-management, 40–41; for taking initiative, 33–34, 44–45; for testing your ideas, 50; to with-draw/continue support, 162–164

Risk: in courageous followership, 18–20, 45; in separation, 155, 160, 168

Roosevelt, Franklin, 74

Rules, 46–47

Rumor control, 59

S

Sabotage, 95

Scandals, 111–112, 116

Scheduling: of leader's time, 57–58; of one's own time, 40–41

Screaming behavior, 102–105; containment of, 139–140, 142; literature on, 183; transformation of, 116–117

Self-assessment, 35, 36–37; in considering separation, 161–162

Self-care, 41–42

Self-management, 40–41, 181

Self-organization: processes of, 119–120; responsibility for, 40–41

Self-worth, 10, 24–25

Separation: and active opposition, 167–169; courage in, 7–8, 147–172; decision to effect, 162–164; versus decision to stay, 171–172; and disavowal, 164–165; due to breaking the trust, 155–157; emotional stakes in, 152–153; establishing criteria for, 157; and evaluating values alignment, 159–161, 163; for exhaustion reasons, 149–150; financial contingencies for, 18–19, 154–155; for group optimization

reasons, 149; and identity issues, 152–153; literature on, 184; by offering to resign, 155–157; for personal growth, 148; based on principle, 150–151, 159–171; reasons for, 148–150; and responsibility, 162–164; self-protection in, 169–171; temporary, of leader from organization, 128–129; and threatening to resign, 157–158, 165

Service: and access to leader, 56–58; and acting in the leader's name, 62–63; by avoiding insularity, 68–70; and breaking the rules, 46–47; by buffering bad news, 58–60; complexity of, 51–53; and conflict among leaders, 75–76; by conserving leader's energy, 53–54; courage in, 7, 12, 51–77; in crisis management, 71–73; by defending the leader, 60; by defining leader's image, 63–64; by encouraging peer relationships for leader, 70–71; by focusing a creative leader, 64–65; gate-keeping responsibilities in, 57–58; to lead-ers, 14, 51–77; literature on, 180; by not pretending expertise, 67–68; to organi-zation, 27; by organizing communication processes, 54–55; by presenting options, 65–67; to self, 14; to stakeholders, 14; by supporting ill leader, 73–74

Shared leadership, 1, 15

Social conditioning, 5, 37–38, 137

Social contract, 4

Soviet Union, 74

Stakeholders, 14

Sununu, John, 112

Support. See Service

Sycophants, 15–16

Systems approach, 125–126

T

Termination. See Separation

Tower, John, 112

Transformation, personal: attitudes towards, 113–114; catalyzing, 123–125; and codependency, 183; and coping with

ABOUT THE AUTHOR

I CAME TO WASHINGTON, D.C., in 1982, another in the never-ending chain of those who see this city as a vehicle for making a difference, large or small. I joined the staff of the Congressional Management Foundation, a nonprofit group that studies management in the U.S. Congress and offers training and consulting to improve existing practices, and subsequently I became its executive director. While the public view of Congress these days is low, there are many dedicated individuals in the institution who are trying to get the work of Congress done. I learned a lot about leader-follower relations from this experience and continue to serve on the foundation's board of directors, as we all try to figure out how to make a difference.

In 1987, I teamed up with Kerry Gleeson, the founder of the Institute for Business Technology (IBT), to open the U.S. branch of this international training and consulting organization. I am president of IBT US. The company has a special niche—improving white-collar productivity at the level of the individual and small work group in the organization. We have a simple but powerful methodology that uses a personalized, on-the-job coaching approach to help participants gain better control of their daunting workloads. This gives me the opportunity to work closely with hundreds of leaders and followers as they struggle with the practical elements of getting their jobs done in very complex organizational settings. We conduct our training programs on-site for scores of Fortune 500 companies, nonprofits, and government agencies.

I also work as an independent consultant in the broader field of organizational and professional development. In this role I audit organizational performance and coach senior executives who want to optimize their performance and that of their teams. As this book goes to press, I am developing leader-follower workshops as vehicles to address the issues I raise in the book.

If you wish to contact me in any of these roles, please do so at 513 Capitol Court N.E., Suite 100, Washington, D.C. 20002; telephone: 202-544-0097; fax: 202-544-6898; home office: 301-933-3752.

Authors, like leaders, need feedback to keep them real. I warmly invite you to send me your experiences in implementing the ideas in this book— what worked, what didn't, what improvements you developed, and what you found helpful in conveying these ideas to your leaders, your colleagues, your followers, your communities, and your children. I am also very interested in written anecdotes about courageous followers. There appears to be almost no literature on acts of courage by followers in relationship to their leaders; I would like to find and document these acts.